CREATIVELY SELF-EMPLOYED

CREATIVELY SELF-EMPLOYED

How Writers and Artists Deal with Career Ups and Downs

Kristen Fischer

iUniverse, Inc.
New York Lincoln Shanghai

Creatively Self-Employed
How Writers and Artists Deal with Career Ups and Downs

iUniverse books may be ordered through booksellers or by contacting:

iUniverse
2021 Pine Lake Road, Suite 100
Lincoln, NE 68512
www.iuniverse.com
1-800-Authors (1-800-288-4677)

ISBN-13: 978-0-595-42154-1 (pbk)
ISBN-13: 978-0-595-86494-2 (ebk)
ISBN-10: 0-595-42154-7 (pbk)
ISBN-10: 0-595-86494-5 (ebk)

Printed in the United States of America

Dedicated to my dear husband, Tim,

who helped me become creatively self-employed.

Contents

Preface

Ever since I quit my 9-to-5 job to pursue a writing career, I've experienced happiness and fulfillment. Paychecks have rolled in as I set my own hours. I've gallivanted out to shop in the middle of the day, or took much-needed breaks to cuddle with my cat, Bobbie, because I wasn't stuck in a cubicle. Heck, I even worked on the beach, writing in the sun.

But then there were weeks where paychecks were "lost in the mail," projects were not coming in, and I had nothing on my precious little fingertips but time. I wondered to myself (and still do, more than I'd like to admit), *Is this really what I should be doing with my life?*

Time is something that I didn't really expect to deal with when I started freelancing, wide-eyed and confident that I'd succeed. It seemed there was either not enough time to get everything done, or that I had too much time on my hands. But with the start of any new business comes down cycles. These are instances when things are slow, and as much as I want to work, the projects just are not there. Then there are times when I put my all into an article, only to have it rejected—again and again. There are 10-hour days I spend sending out resumes in speed sprees to make sure I do not lapse in projects. I try to find innovative ways to market my services. I attempt to keep track of finances. Trying to mull up new ideas for fresh material.

The truth is, I still struggle to stay afloat whether it comes to finding the bacon, dealing with rejection and staying motivated. I even doubt my ability to *write* sometimes, and I still worry that I'll sink. Every once in a while, however, I'll run into someone who tells me that I have their "dream job." I sit back from the laptop, pull Bobbie into my lap and realize how lucky I am to be living this life—this *authentic* life. That's when I know that this *is* what I should be doing, that this is my life's work.

It's authentic not only because I'm following my innate talent of writing. It's authentic because I'm daring to make it on my own; to put myself out there for all to see. I'm daring to make a living based on my flair for words. In fact, there is nothing normal about the life I lead. It's scary and wonderful, thrilling and rewarding. It breaks me and completes me. It gives me strength. Most importantly, it makes me *alive*. There are so many emotions associated with knowing that I'm living my dream—so I *know* I'm really living.

That's why I decided to document the lives of writers, designers, painters, artists and other creative types who have taken the plunge into self-employment. They're living off their talents and telling all about it. And I find it fascinating. I also find the message of this book to be imperative; many creatives may quit when they experience a down cycle. And that does not mean their creative venture isn't meant to be; it just means they need to see that ups and downs are normal in the creative life. And what better way to help other creatives realize they're not alone than to show them others who have experienced the same things and still came out shining?

The goal of this book is to provide comfort and understanding for those who are in the midst of doubt. Maybe you've been in business for a while and are worried that you won't find new clients. Or you're still struggling with the solitude of working alone. Perhaps the financial weight of sparse or infrequent paychecks has you in a panic. Whatever you're feeling, you'll hear how others are dealing with the very same things as you are.

For seasoned creatives, this book will help you further understand how to thrive in a sometimes-uncertain industry and how to learn from your work patterns to optimize your performance. You'll see how to improve your self-esteem in your work. Maybe you'll pick up new ideas. Maybe you'll rekindle the fire that got you where you are in the first place.

Whatever you get from this book, it's bound to remind you that the lives we lead are special. That what you're doing is brave. And that you can continue to do it with a little support. That no matter what you face, there are other people out there in the same situation. And it's about time people heard our stories.

Acknowledgements

I would like to officially thank …

All of the participants, whose honesty will pave the way for a better understanding of creative careers, and why those who choose them are so special.

Dan Galimidi, for your design help and patience.

Kristen King, for wordsmithing my jumble of a book and being an all-around cool girl.

My friends, who make my life fun and crazy. Now you know someone who wrote a book *and* won a car—ha!

Tine, for being my Canadian cheerleader. I'm so glad we "met."

Norma, who helps me to grow more positive every day.

My in-laws—Dad, Mom, Chris, Carri, LaLa, Alison and Ryan and the rest of the family—who support me as I am one of their own.

My cat, Bobbie, for keeping the desk covered in cat fur—as it should be.

My family, who make me proud to be part of it.

My grandmother, who I know watches from above every day.

My sister, Danielle, for being the best big "didder."

My mother, who taught me that life *is* beautiful.

My husband, Tim, my very best friend, whose love makes me a better person.

And God, for His unconditional wisdom and strength.

Chapter 1

✦

Freelance Freedom

I believe there is a very personal reward for those who venture into the creative self-employment industry. Whether you are a writer, a painter, a sculptor, a musician, a graphic artist or a jewelry maker, those of us who have chosen the creative life can all agree that the freedom is perhaps the biggest draw to the job.

That's not to say that there aren't difficulties associated with creative self-employment. It is such complexities that led me to write this book in hopes that by exposing these hardships—along with the joys—we can gain strength to continue on our genuine paths and excel in our careers. Do keep in mind that *creative* self-employment bears its own challenges and triumphs.

But before we go there, I'd like to start off the book by going back to our roots. You know that top-of-the-world feeling that came after you took the plunge into creative self-employment? Sure, you were worried about paying your bills and finding adequate health insurance. But the day you pranced out of your 9-to-5 job, aside from the fear, what were you feeling? Bliss? Probably so. Fear? Definitely. Regardless, there was the spark that led you to where you are.

The *freedom.* It came in various forms for each of us. Some relished taking off an afternoon for leisure. Others found bliss working in their pajamas. Some took pleasure in sleeping in on days they would have otherwise set the alarm clock for 6 a.m.

Me? I have to say that the first time I just *sat* in Starbucks in the middle of a weekday gave me chills. Though I felt like I should be back at my 9-to-5 job, trapped behind a desk, I also knew that being able to work on my own terms felt euphoric. I always used to ask myself when I'd stop in the café after work at night and think, *What do those "Starbucks people" do in there all day?* And then, one day, I knew. One day, I was one of those people. Maybe not the ones who sit and read, or just watch people. But those people who are working there, because they can work anywhere they want.

Somehow, work doesn't seem like such a drag in the midst of floating jazz music and foamy drinks. For me, it was a dream of sorts. And finally, one day soon after I left that 9-to-5 job, I was there, finding out what it was like to do my copywriting work from that café. Am I being paid by Starbucks to promote them? No. The place just represents freedom and relaxation to me, and it is a good analogy to illustrate my point of feeling liberated.

As I flopped into the green velvet chair and sipped my warm chai—in a ceramic mug instead of a cardboard to-go cup—I was amazed. I could work where I wanted. I could work *wherever* I wanted. I could take breaks when I wanted. I could type a sentence and spend the rest of the afternoon reveling in exotic paintings, whiffing in the aroma of coffee. Not to say I was a goof-off; I was, and am, *very* serious about my work. But it was the fact that I *could* do all of those frivolous things if I wanted to. I had more time to because I didn't have a commute. And I didn't have a commute because I was free.

I had taken a dive into a sea of doubt, but the independence was a safe feeling for me. I savored it as I began my career as a writer. I

knew there would be ups and downs; but for that one afternoon—
and every subsequent time I escape to any of my "safe places"—I
remember why I chose the path that I did.

First off, I wanted to write. I was ready to scrap my years as a
report writer for an environmental company. And move on from a
short stint as a municipal reporter. I was ready to write whatever I
wanted to. I knew I could make money in the field of copywriting,
which would afford me the time to pitch magazines and compile a
book. The simple art of writing was the passion. It still is. Although
I must say, the dream of becoming an *author*—as opposed to just a
writer—was always my ultimate goal.

I chose the path because I knew I could handle it. I was an independent worker. I thrived when I was in a comfortable environment
complete with soft music and the smell of java. I didn't have to rot
in a cubicle in corporate America to make a lot of money. I had the
drive to succeed and the willingness to do whatever it took to get
there. After months of building my business, and my portfolio, I
was ready to be on my own. Wherever that was—and the fact that
this exciting lifestyle would bring me something new every day had
major appeal.

I would pick and choose my clients and the types of projects I
would undertake. I would use my assertiveness to drum up new
business. I'd create attractive, hip marketing materials for myself. I'd
submit resumes to companies that weren't even hiring. And I would
write and make a real living.

That's exactly what happened. And sometimes, even *I* am still
amazed by it all.

I'm 28. I wake up when my body says it's done sleeping, instead
of when the alarm clock mandates it. I get new clients every week.
Sometimes I work in my pajamas. I work diligently on projects that
pay me quadruple the rate I used to make. I take days off when I feel

like it. I've built up my experience and ventured into exciting new realms of the writing and editing world. I've made it.

And I always think back to that first day of creative self-employment, when I sat at Starbucks. When I learned what the "Starbucks people" do. Sure, some of them have weekdays off but still work full-time jobs. Some of them don't work at all. But others live a lifestyle where they can go to a place they love to do their work. They are their own bosses.

Without the confines of a 9-to-5 job, I was at a place that I'd dreamed of. Of course Starbucks' appeal has mildly worn off. Plus, the coffee prices are a little high. I love my home office now more than anything, and completed it with an espresso machine for the times when I don't want to leave the house. But regardless of where I am and what I do, I'm free. No matter what it took to get me here, I've made it. Ask any creatively self-employed person and they'll agree: There is no better feeling.

How I Got My Start

For me, writing was always in the cards. I think I knew in the fourth grade when I was selected to represent my elementary school at writer's camp. It was a small feat, but a profound achievement. My family recognized my way with words instantly; my mother a strong supporter from the start.

As my schooling continued, I was not sure what I wanted to do with my life, but I knew I wanted to attend college. Like most girls my age, I had an obsession with saving dolphins (it was during the tuna scare, so the jumping on the Greenpeace bandwagon was easy), so I ended up majoring in environmental science. I never thought to major in English or writing; I never thought anyone could make a viable living from it.

I dreaded the look and feel of completing my field work in the dirt, and chemistry made me squeamish. But when it came to my law and policy classes where I was writing reports and essays, I excelled. I took all of my electives in creative nonfiction and auto-biographical writing, figuring it was a fun hobby.

About a week before I graduated—probably like most students—I started to realize that I didn't want to use my degree. I did try to get a job in my field, but was unsure if I even really wanted to pursue anything related to environmental studies. So when environmental opportunities did not pan out (they wanted people who liked dirt) I went with what came naturally—writing.

For a year and a half, I was a newspaper reporter. Wondering if I should try to use my degree before continuing to write, I ventured into environmental consulting; eventually landing a job that gave me the title of environmental scientist without my having to venture out into the mud. I worked as a technical report writer. I was still crafting words—and learning how to write technically—but still miserable.

When I was fed up with the job, I decided that I would somehow continue in communications. That was when I had built up some business on the side and chose to supplement it with a part-time job as a copy editor at a newspaper. Yep, I went back to the newsroom.

Now I'm in my late 20s, and I've been in business for nearly three years. It wasn't easy. After a year as a copy editor at a newspaper, I moved to a job at home that would let me devote more time and resources to my growing client list. At one point, my part-time job fell through and my copywriting side business wasn't enough. It *was* enough, however, to make me anxious. Not sure if I was ready to take the plunge and work completely on a freelance basis, I had no other choice. Sure, I could have gotten another full-time job, but I was on the path to "breaking free," and didn't want to take a step back. So with the support of my husband, Tim, I plunged anyway.

I've come up for air many times, debated rushing back to shore—but I've never left the water of creative self-employment. It just feels too good.

*   *   *

As you read the stories in this book, I am sure you will identify with many—if not all—of them. Appendix C includes website addresses of the creatively self-employed people I interviewed. It will give you a better glimpse into each of their businesses. And now, let's find out what it's *really* like to be creatively self-employed from people who know best.

Freedom Fibers

Denise M. Cawley is a fiber artist, quilter, fabric dyer and teacher. As the president of Pizzazz Studios, a Wisconsin-based company, she also sells art supplies and teaches artistic workshops. And if that weren't enough, Cawley also handles marketing for a number of creative organizations.

But self-employed success didn't happen overnight for her. With non-profit organization experience under her belt, she advanced to working for a large company. It was there that Cawley had complete health benefits and gained a lot of knowledge and experience managing projects.

On the side, she started teaching workshops about color theory, quilting and fabric dyeing. It felt good to use her natural talents and do something she deeply enjoyed. "By choice, I made a deliberate decision go after my dreams," says Cawley, who felt "very called by the universe" to pursue a fabric business shortly after. "I felt like the sky opened up and God, goddess and Buddha were all saying, 'Hey, this is what you are supposed to do with your life,'" Cawley recalls.

"Once I tasted that purposeful life, it was hard to go back to work every day and do things that were not satisfying."

She was showing artwork in galleries at this point, which gave her the confidence boost she needed to seriously consider taking her creative dream a step further and becoming self-employed. But for many people, taking a creative step, as small as it is, can feel like a dive—*into ice water.*

"I thought the money I made from teaching would just gradually build up to the same level I made at my 'real' job," says Cawley, who at the time believed that quitting would be easy. The truth was, she couldn't build up her business enough by only having evenings and weekends to devote to it—she needed to be available during the week. Something had to give. Cawley's partner was supportive in her decision to "just quit," which is exactly what she did. Talk about guts; most of us have spent months—even years—planning our escapes.

People always think that having a creative career is easy. They imagine venturing out of their corporate job for the last time, walking out of the building without the thought of ever turning back, delightfully taking the air in, smiling and speeding home with the radio volume high. For most creatively self-employed people, those first steps outside the building include gasps for air in panic, and an overwhelming desire to run back inside.

"I remember crying all the way out my last day," says Cawley, who worried then about what she would do without the structure that her "real" job provided. She feared not being able to take care of her partner. Then the guilt piled on. So she worked all the time; taking any opportunity she could to make the money she needed to pay bills and pay off the debt she accrued to make the move. "I was always worried, but that fear was a good motivator to make it work."

Three years later, Cawley has found that she wouldn't have it any other way. Now she is able to pick and choose her projects. The debt is still there, but she's chipping away at it. Her partner has supported her as she advances her creative dream. She works in her pajamas sometimes, too. (As a side note, you won't believe just how *many* people who participated in this book cited "working in my jammies" as a major job perk!) She's made it happen, for sure. And for all the hardships that still ensue, it's living a purposeful, enjoyable life that makes any adversity in the future well worth living fully in the present.

Cawley's story sounds like many of those who have ventured into creative self-employment. Most of us did not just stumble into it, but had to pay our dues in steady, 40-hour-a-week jobs. I refer to them here as 9-to-5's. They're the kind of full-time jobs that most people have, which require working a set amount of hours in-house for a company. They aren't all boring or horrible; but for most of us who ventured into self-employment, we dread going back to them like the plague.

Michael Katz, a marketing consultant from Massachusetts who launched Blue Penguin Development in 2000, left his job in a Nike-like way. He just did it. "I walked into my boss's office one day and resigned," recalls Katz, whose business helps clients increase sales by showing them how to market themselves. He specializes in electronic newsletters. "I had been telling friends and family that I wasn't going to turn 40 in a company. I left two months before my birthday." That was pretty much it.

"I wanted the freedom to just do what I wanted and to build a business around what I was really good at," says Katz. "For me, success is about blending work and leisure, so that the concept of a 'job' goes away. I try to work as much as feels comfortable and don't find [that] working more or harder has anything to do with how much money I earn."

But not everyone can "just quit." Many of us lined up our careers on the side and left our steady jobs when we felt that our side business was strong enough to make transition possible, like Mary Stewart-Pellegrini, the managing director of organizational consulting firm the Stewart Management Group in Illinois. She built quite the nest egg before she went out on her own, planning for *five years* to start her business.

"Advanced planning is critical," Stewart-Pellegrini says. "I had money saved, a clear focus for my business, a couple of well-paying clients, a good lawyer and a terrific accountant. My personal challenge was to manage the money I earned, to invest the profit wisely, to protect my personal energy while also learning how to develop new client relationships, to market and sell products and services, to ideate and collaborate with others and to select the right projects."

And did it pay off? Absolutely! Her business is thriving as her impressive client list increases. "It was hard work … but the planning made it very worthwhile," says Stewart-Pellegrini.

Not all of us built up clientele for a while before we dove in, either. Some of us ventured into part-time employment while we built our dream careers. Heck, many of us still have a part-time gig to keep the money coming in so we don't lose sleep over whether we will be able to pay our bills every month. And still others fell into self-employment after losing their jobs and having nowhere else to turn but to themselves.

We all got here from somewhere. We all have interesting stories. And we can all deal better with the challenges if we listen to these stories. So now, we're all creatively self-employed. And if you thought the hardest thing was giving two weeks notice to your 9-to-5, you were probably mistaken. Our daily lives can be riddled with excitement and fear over sharing our work, finding new clients and making ends meet.

Let's look at yet another person who dove into this career. Though your story may not be similar to this next one (which I found extremely profound), you can still remember the feelings of freedom that came along with going into creative self-employment. And by sharing these stories, hopefully you can rekindle those feelings to propel yourself through difficult times.

From Tragedy to Triumph

Getting into creative self-employment wasn't as easy for Kristine Di Grigoli Paige, an artist from New Jersey. Having always experimented with independent working, in 2000 she created a gallery out of her home where she offered private art lessons for children.

But soon after September 11, 2001, her just-across-the-Hudson-River town was devastated, and so was her business. She was forced to close her doors and return to a 9-to-5 job.

"The towers fell and I found myself painting dark images of Afghanistan women with dark crimson backgrounds," says Paige, who at the time used her personal art to express the fears she had for the United States.

In 2002, she picked up the pieces and founded The Sound and Vision Show. She started painting live to rock bands, acoustic soloists, jazz acts and other musicians at popular music venues such as The Knitting Factory in New York City. "I sold a few paintings and gained some Web clients. I produced over 50 shows in two years," recalls Paige. But she had to go back to 9-to-5 work again for steady income. "The shows simply were not enough for me to live on. It was fun, but felt as if it wasn't enough at a certain point."

It wasn't until 2005 that she got commercial space in nearby Hoboken, New Jersey, and took her project one step further, starting The Sound and Vision Gallery. Having the gallery space has allowed her to capitalize on the studio, bringing in additional income. "I can show off my artwork in the gallery area, I can rent out my studio space for other artists to use, I can offer drawing classes, paint live to music and so on," says Paige, who is elated to be in her new creative space with the liberty she has always craved. "I can dress as I please, eat when I want to, check my e-mail all day long, come and go as I please. I'm free."

Tragedy turned into triumph for Paige. Sometimes when life's little calamities hit, it gives us proof that a new door opens when one closes.

∗   ∗   ∗

September 11, 2001 also affected Beth Erickson's writing business. But she knows the fallout had nothing to do with her talent. Tragic events—and even rising gas prices—can affect marketing budgets, which in turn affect our workloads.

"Sometimes outside forces dictate how much work will come in," says the Minnesota-based creator of www.filbertpublishing.com and *Writing, Etc.*, an industry e-zine. She says that the only way for writers to protect themselves (we can assume that goes for artists and designers as well) is to maintain more than one income stream. For Erickson, she's done that with her book endeavors and copywriting business. "There's plenty to do," says Erickson.

She brings up a valid point, one that I would like to make early on. For a lot of creatives, having a steady gig helps. The people in this book do not have full-time steady jobs, but some do some part-time work. It helps you get—and stay—on your feet, and there's nothing wrong with it. For many, it is the perfect way to slowly break free and be financially responsible when launching a creative business. Even I have some regular work from a creative agency that gives me flexible hours and the ability to guarantee some income. I do not rely solely on projects from new clients all of the time; sometimes it's good to have a working relationship on an ongoing basis. No one said creative self-employment meant having new and exciting projects that you like all of the time. Some of my continuing work as a copywriter is not on the most interesting side, but it pays well.

The difference between creatives and those tied to a full-time job is that it's easy—and common—to switch gigs. As long as you can keep money coming in to make a living, opportunities for creatives are limitless.

The Back and Forth of It All

Creative self-employment is not steady for everyone. Sometimes, you have to bounce around to land firmly on your feet. Melanie Negrin, a copywriter and managing director of Merocuné Marketing and Public Relations, has gone back and forth from freelancing to the corporate world for years. After the birth of her first daughter, she had to go back to a full-time job for a corporation. But she used the opportunity to build up her credentials as a professional writer.

"Often money and the need to survive tempt me to go back full-time," says Negrin, who lives in New Jersey. "But I find it hard to interview for a full-time position when my heart is in freelancing and building my own business."

Build her own business she did. After the birth of her second child, Negrin felt confident about her success as a self-employed creative. She started her company and made the business-savvy move of turning previous employers into clients. Her business has a niche for charities, which is where her passion lies: in helping others. But Negrin was able to help herself, too. By being smart about finances as she raised her family, she took the time to establish a strong foundation for her current business and has been met with success.

Accidental Bliss

When Craig Poulton, president of Web design firm InWeb Media in Canada, did not have the money to pay a designer to create a website he wanted to start, he began to learn about multimedia and design in his Montreal home. Learning the design program was a good start, but he didn't find it challenging enough. So he applied to work as a designer for a small graphic design firm. He only had a little experience, so he decided to create his own samples. "I created a few websites and copied them to a floppy disk," says Poulton. "Not only was the company impressed with my work, but I beat out 20 other applicants for the job."

After working at the firm for more than two years he was promoted to marketing director, but Poulton found that he wanted to expand his horizons and get into a job with more responsibilities. He took a 9-to-5 job as the director of business development for an Internet company in Toronto. The company went bankrupt after he'd been there only six months.

That's when Poulton found his way—in the midst of an uncertain situation. More than three years later, Poulton now employs five workers and runs his own Web design firm. And he couldn't be happier. "This line of work allows me to experience new types of businesses and new and dynamic people," says Poulton. "I've learned more about myself in the last five years than I did in my lifetime."

It's clear to see that what could have been a devastating blow turned into a huge opportunity. Instead of sitting at his 9-to-5 job waiting to break out and go freelance, sometimes creative self-employment just finds people as the only way to bring in money. When it turns into a profitable business, even more rewards follow.

Something similar happened to Tamar Wallace, a designer from Massachusetts. She was working as an in-house designer for a real estate company when she heard that the business across the street had lost its designer. "I called them to inquire about the position, but only to use it as leverage to get a raise at my current job," says Wallace. During her conversation with the other company, she learned that it was looking to outsource the position. They asked her if she would be interested in interviewing for the job.

With less than a week to put together a portfolio, develop a price structure and mentally prepare for the interview, she dove into the opportunity, and wound up landing the contract. "Six months later, they had me so busy, I had to quit my job, and there I was— self-employed. I often tell people it happened by accident," says Wallace. Accident or fate? Regardless, she loves her life as a creative freelancer, running one-woman design business TAMAR Graphics, which grew to a multi-person team within five years.

"I consider myself very lucky. I have a strong family that continues to inspire and support me, I get to do what I love for a living, and I get to stay home to watch my son grow up," says Wallace. "The bad times can be very, very bad. But everything else makes it so worth it."

The *Real* Simple Life

Jeff Wilson, a narrator, host, and actor who has appeared on HGTV and the DIY Network, would agree that living creatively self-employed is worth it. The Ohio resident, who calls himself "Jeff Wilson, Regular Guy," has been able to put aside a lot of the usual fears about money because he lives a frugal and simple life. (In many ways, I think he is what we all envision self-employment to be like: great work and simple living. It's not quite like this for most of us, but his stance on creative self-employment was one I found extremely refreshing.)

Wilson describes creative self-employment as a delicate balance. He strives to make sure he has time with his family whether he's swamped or in a slump. "I can be just as anxious about too much work as no work," says Wilson. "I guess it really depends on how you measure success … If it's money you're after, there's never enough. We have always valued free time and the ability to choose what we're going to do with each day."

He has been able to stay self-employed with the help of his wife's frugality. "[It] has lessened the anxiety you get from too little work, and kept us from having to accept too much work," adds Wilson. To him, self-employment has given him the opportunity *not* to conform to the consumerism of most Americans. When people tell him it must be nice to be home in the middle of the day (isn't that so annoying?), he tells them that he works part-time for part-time pay and makes the rest of his income from what he does at home with the time he saves from not working. "We do our own cooking, cleaning, home improvement, auto mechanics, children's day care, and a host of other things most people pay to have done," Wilson says.

So does he miss anything about 9-to-5 life?

"I'd say that I miss the camaraderie of the office, but I remember how even that degenerated to sniping when things got hectic. What we have given up in structure and predictability, we've gained in freedom and variety of experience," says Wilson.

So what's best about his life as a creatively self-employed person?

"We've had almost 15 years of self-employment, and we've spent that time well. I haven't missed too many breakfasts or dinners with my kids, and we've made sure to take as much time for vacations each year as shooting schedules and money allow," he says. "You really can't replace the walks to school or to piano lessons with the kids. I'll be telling myself that as I work my way through those retirement years!"

Exploring New Horizons

Mick Quinn, an author and former Wall Street CEO, once worked for a successful start-up company. He had experienced loneliness despite being surrounded by friends and colleagues. When the gig turned into a 9-to-5 job, Quinn decided to move into a more inspirational career. "It was slightly unnerving to leave, but trust goes a long way," says Quinn. "9-to-5 offers a false security that is obvious to an entrepreneur."

Now he is living in Europe and busy traveling internationally, spreading the messages in his book, *Power and Grace: The Four Insights of Authentic Joy*. What's best about following his dream of exploring spirituality and writing a groundbreaking book about it? For Quinn, it's the simple things. "Sometimes I get up at 5.30 a.m. to start work. At that time, the sun is rising over the fields and old vineyard here. There is a light mist and it is quite still," he says. "Just to be able to see that whenever I choose is more than enough inspiration to continue this work."

Your Own Identity

Another plus to the creative self-employment is the individuality it allows. Not because we can simply create something that no one else has, but because we can put our name to it; as opposed to slapping a large corporate byline on the work.

Billy Bussey, a digital producer from California, says he's fortunate to be creatively self-employed because his name is attached to the work he creates, unlike if he were a staff or in-house developer. "I've been able to create a name for myself and sell it, which I couldn't do as an employee of someone else," he says. "My portfolio is strictly mine."

I notice that the same is true in my field of copywriting. Snag a big-name client, and the power and good reputation that company has sort of rubs off on your name. Plus, it looks darn fine in your ever-important portfolio.

Working for yourself lets you create your own image as well. Whether your business cards are plain-Jane black and white or your website is filled with color splashes and funky animated designs, it's okay in the creative world. Most businesses like it when we express our creativity while keeping it professional. They've come to depend on us for a breath of fresh air. (So *that's* why they hire out contractors!)

There is no need for navy suits and ties, either. Business casual? For me, only during meetings. The rest of my wardrobe has been transformed into a hodgepodge of comfortable athletic pants, jeans, tank tops, cozy sweaters and flip flops. Works for me. Most creatives have their own style as well, and the ability to work in jammies or dress in über-professional attire suits us each differently. It's part of the freedom, and oh, it's *sweet* freedom.

The Flexibility of Corporate Life

Cheri Larson, president and founder of Azante Jewelry, feels inspired by her work and the freedom it gives her. The Wisconsin-based designer started an advertising agency and graphic design firm. As a mother, she longed for the flexibility of her own business.

"I grew up with parents who were self-employed, so in many respects, it felt quite natural to own my own business," says Larson, whose direct sales company specializes in handcrafted sterling silver and gemstone jewelry. Though she logs long hours, she can work around her kids' schedules and still has time to take business very seriously. But she admits that there is never a time she's not thinking about her job—and she doesn't mind. She knows it is part of the creative self-employment process. "In many jobs, you are able to put your work aside and go home. Being self-employed is not just a job—it's a lifestyle and a state of mind," notes Larson. "Creative individuals not only desire, but *need* to have an environment where they can express their talents. A restrictive corporate environment does not allow creative types to break out of the box and explore their talents. The key is being able to harness the creativity and market your service or product effectively."

So when Larson left the corporate environment and went into self-employment, she was thrilled. For her, it was a natural transition. (She also has a very supportive husband, which I know from personal experience is a big help.)

"It was very exhilarating, knowing that I was in charge of my own destiny," she says.

Still, there are others out there who are not so quick when it comes to stepping away from the water cooler and fluorescent lights. There are good and bad aspects of life on either side of the corporate door; but creatives know that they're best off away from cubicle life. What ensues after one follows that dream can be difficult.

But just because it can be hard doesn't mean it's not worth it.

The Illusion of 9-to-5 Work

Marisa Haedike, an artist from California, was happy to break free from her 9-to-5 job as an interior designer. Now she's selling artwork and offering free podcasts about creative living via her website (see Chapter 10 for more about these fabulous resources). Aside from the thrill of being on her own, Haedike has an important insight into creative self-employment: She says a 9-to-5 full-time job only provides the *illusion* of financial security, because workers can be fired at any moment.

"When you work for yourself you are building something that is solely yours, that you will always have if you choose to," Haedike says. "It is rewarding in a way I had never known existed and it is so worth it, even when the fears sneak up on you." She says creatives struggle not because of the 9-to-5 versus creative self-employment scenario, but because of their fears as opposed to the peace and sense of security they want. "The hardest thing [about creative self-employment] is trusting that even though you don't know what's coming next, it's all working out for your best interest," she says. "Working a [9-to-5] job is really the same experience, you just have the illusion that you know what you will be doing tomorrow."

I never thought about it before she mentioned it, but it's true. Every so often, I wonder what life would be like if I got a cubicle and a nice steady paycheck. Most of the people I interviewed for this book had the same thoughts.

Sure, being creatively self-employed feels a little less sturdy than the comfort of a 9-to-5 job; but that doesn't mean you can't succeed at this unique career lifestyle. When I have those thoughts, I remember the emotions attached to working 9-to-5. Even when the job wasn't horrible, I still did not enjoy the monotony of it all, and the inflexibility. And yes, my head was on the chopping block a few times, so I know it wasn't any more secure than what I'm doing now. As a writer, I've secured business which makes me feel more secure about the relationships I've built. I trust myself to continue my business. So it may not seem it, but when you work professionally at your business, you actually have *more* job security.

Why Creatives Are So Extraordinary

In these stories is the essence of what this book is all about. It is for those out there who dare not only to dream, but also to act on their aspirations. It is for those who wish to venture outside the confines of security, for those who bid farewell to comfortable health benefits, decent paychecks and office social lives.

Creatively Self-Employed: How Writers and Artists Deal with Career Ups and Downs will not tell you how to muster up the courage to leave your 9-to-5 job to chase your fantasy of watercolor painting. If you're reading this, chances are you're out of a "real" job, sitting in your living room (having spent your savings on paint) and staring at a blank canvas. Maybe you're doing well in business, but still struggle with the feelings associated with creative self-employment. These include fear, doubt—and even elation to be living your dream. (Yes, success can be difficult to cope with as well.)

The truth is that pursuing a creative dream is not easy. But there are resources out there to help people do it. As a freelance writer who took a plunge similar to Cawley's, "getting out" was actually the *easy* part for me. But it left me wondering, on a day when work wasn't coming in and I stared at my laptop … *What's supposed to happen next? Is something wrong with me? Am I really a legitimate copywriter? How can I get more clients? Should I really be doing this in the first place?* After all, the very nature of being out on your own can feel *so* uneasy.

It seems that our society is all about encouraging us to do what makes us happy. But after we make the bold choice to pursue our creative dreams, what lies ahead? Often, feelings of self-doubt, anxiety and even depression can follow. Sometimes our support systems are gone when we kiss goodbye steady paychecks. And it's not that we're not doing what we are meant to—it's just hard making a living alone, no matter who you are or how strong your business is. There will always be struggles when all aspects of your business rest on your shoulders.

So to that, I say remember that what you're doing is truly extraordinary. Look around you—you are in a scenario that only few truly understand. And remember that you're not arrogant for realizing you are in a unique career. What you do is sort of elite;

you're not better than anyone else but you're doing something that many others wouldn't dare to. And because of that, you have to give yourself credit.

Realizing this will help you out when the rest of the world doesn't seem to understand the trials of your job. A key factor in getting through the hard times was giving yourself permission to feel upset (or happy, too!) It is okay to experience the feelings that will come with creative self-employment. *Many people may not understand because they haven't dared to live their dream.*

Come along, this is where the true beauty of a creative career lies: in the unknowns, the twists, turns, trials and triumphs. It's in the real voices of men and women brave enough to take a giant risk, and those who have been brave enough to tell about it. And it's in the inspirational moments that somehow only hit when you're working in your pajamas … or just sitting at Starbucks.

CREATIVE PROFILE
Elaina Loveland
Writer and Consultant
Alexandria, Virginia

Getting Started
Elaina Loveland is a former editor of the Journal of College Admission. An active freelance writer, she is the author of *Creative Colleges: A Guide for Student Actors, Artists, Dancers, Musicians, and Writers.*

Breaking into Business
"Thinking of the arts as a business is the key to making your passion your profession," says Elaina. "The most important thing a creative person can do to actually make a living in the arts is to start branding themselves as an artist as early as possible. The earlier you start accepting that you need to intersect the arts with the business world, the sooner you will be able to start making money doing it."

Putting on Professionalism
Elaina recommends creating a business plan with three-month, six-month, and one-year goals; joining a local chamber of commerce and networking with local art groups; reading business books geared towards entrepreneurs; and starting or joining a support group for creative businesspeople.

For more information about Elaina, visit www.elainaloveland.com.

CHAPTER 2

✦

PUTTING IT OUT THERE

I think it's true that every good artist doubts his or her work sometimes, especially in the beginning of his or her career. Growing confident in your craft includes getting approval from others, and the only way to get that is to put your work "out there" for all to see, read and experience.

Once an artist has gotten past his or her first gallery show, or sold so many paintings, there is a natural acceptance of their work—and themselves, because the work is so personal—that creatives gain. They see that others appreciate their talent, which confirms their adoration for their own unique style. For writers, it comes when that magazine editor agrees that a query letter will make a great article. They see that someone else thinks their work is good, and roll with the newfound confidence, sometimes having to walk the plank with each new painting or piece of prose they create. After a while, walking out on the wobbly piece of wood isn't as hard—it gets easier each time creatives go.

But it does take time.

The hardest part of our careers may not have been giving up steady paychecks or water-cooler discussions at work. Sometimes it's having the courage to step out on our own and show our talents, even if the people closest to us discourage us every step of the way. Whether we feel as if we are walking the plank or stepping out on a highway into rush-hour traffic, there is a threshold of fear we must overcome when we display our work for all to see. There is a dread associated with putting it out there, and a fear of facing rejection when we do. That fear can come with showcasing our talent, or even marketing ourselves (that is also putting yourself "out there").

Stepping out onto the plank gets easier each time you do it. You may have to do it repeatedly. But I guess the biggest note of advice I have regarding self-promotion is that it *does* take time to get better at building the confidence needed to thrive as a creatively self-employed person.

Separating Yourself from Your Product

To run a successful business, you have to market yourself and put your product or work out for all to see. For many creatives, there is a lot of fear associated with doing this.

Gail Rhyno, a beach-glass jewelry maker from Canada, knows that the fear of rejection for some artists starts with the dread of sharing their work. Every time she sends a product sample to a store, there is a chance that it won't be accepted, Rhyno says. "The problem for me is separating the reasons for rejection and recognizing that it is not always connected with my product," she notes.

She says that if a store has just purchased all of their merchandise for the upcoming season, she knows they simply are not able to purchase jewelry from her, which is not the same as them outright rejecting her jewelry. "That is a rejection, but not of my work. I try to keep that in mind," she adds. "And you do feel vulnerable, because let's face it, you are asking people if they like your product, which can translate into 'Do you like me?' if you are not careful."

She makes perfect sense here. Sometimes it's hard to separate a rejection of one's work from a rejection in general. In her case, a store may not have any more money for inventory, so they can't purchase more merchandise even if they love it. For a writer, a particular magazine may not *hate* the story submitted; they may not be covering that topic at the time the article is submitted. This is the first thing to remember about putting your work out there and facing rejection: The work may not be rejected because of its content. Still new to her company, Rhyno, in my opinion, is off to a strong start with her practical mindset.

"When I do not hear an immediate response to a product sample I have sent out, I quickly assume it is negative," she says. "But I am sure that as my technique improves and I feel more established in my craft, this response will disappear."

Rhyno illustrates a valuable point. If you're afraid of rejection, you just have to keep in mind when you step onto the plank or the roadway that people aren't rejecting *you*. It's a subjective world out there. There are many avenues for creative work to shine. And if at first you do not succeed ... you have to try, try again. At least if you want to eat or make rent, right?

*   *   *

If I told you I was a chronic people-pleaser, I wouldn't be lying. As a perfectionist and workaholic, I strive to do my best. And as a result, I've had to learn to go easier on myself when putting my work out there. When I have completed a project and the client isn't happy, I try to remember that I can always fix things. Sometimes a simple extra round of editing does the trick. I realize all hope is not lost, and it's not really realistic to assume the client will adore my first draft. The point is, when we know we can make things right in the end, why do we so fear letting go? The work can come back to us; it will all be okay.

Calvin Lee, creative director of branding and identity firm Mayhem Studios, in California, knows all about trying to please clients. He doesn't struggle so much with putting his work out there, but he puts his all into his work to make it his best—and to avoid client disapproval. "You want everyone to like your work, but you can't please everyone," says Lee. "As long as you know you've done good work and you did your best to solve your clients' problems, you should feel good."

Easy to say, I bet you're thinking. Or at least you did when you heard that as a beginning freelancer. But it is true. And as Lee says, if you have been in the industry for some time, rejection is just part of the job description.

For all you fearful artists out there, let's deal with one psychosis at a time. *Just put it out there.* We'll learn how to cope with the rejection potential in the next chapter. For now, let's explore more of the common fears that cause artists to clam up and never fulfill their true potential.

Approaching Others

Fear is a strong de-motivator for many creatives. Take Marianne Roosa, a graphic designer and illustrator from the Netherlands. She believes that success is all about who you know these days, and confesses she is not very good about approaching people. Now that she is on her own, she knows that seeking out new clients is a vital aspect of the business—but for her, it's very stressful. "I really need to get over my fear to approach people," says Roosa. "If I could do that and be more confident about my work, then I know I could have more success."

I have to agree with her. Sometimes I see my laptop as a shield from the rest of the world. After all, it's easy to sit in an encouraging office complete with notes from supporters and pretty pictures on the wall while creating prose at my leisure. But then the business aspect is tied in—I have to make money to afford to create in seclusion. This includes continually marketing myself to get new gigs and add more to my portfolio, which, in turn, helps me get more work.

Creatives need to put their art aside at times and learn the business side of it all if they really want to thrive. I've watched too many people not take their business seriously enough and end up going back to 9-to-5 life. And hey, for some people that's okay. But chances are, if you're reading this, you want to do anything but. When you develop a strong business sense, putting your work out there will not be as hard. You'll know the playing field and understand that you have to be in it to win it. Or, like I said, at least to make rent.

A No-Nonsense Approach

I like Tera Leigh's outlook on putting one's work out there. You'll read in Chapter 3 about dealing with the rejection that can ensue, but basically she is no-nonsense when it comes to getting over the fear.

"This is a business," says Leigh, an artist from Oklahoma who has written numerous books and magazine articles. "Put on your 'big girl panties' and create a business plan and a marketing plan, and show your work." Her view is valuable for all creatives who want to run a business because she cuts to essence of succeeding with a creative business. Though there are unique challenges, it *is* still a business.

"When I was an attorney, I had to worry about invoices, etc.," she says. "If you want to be a professional artist, then you are a businessperson and you are going to have to do those things, or get enough money saved to hire someone to do it. If you don't want to do it, then don't go into business."

Her advice applies to all people, whether they want to be an artist, author, attorney, own a store, or run any other kind of business. "You aren't exempt because you are creative," Leigh points out. "If you want to make a living, then you have to view your work as a product, not as an extension of yourself. If someone doesn't like your work, it doesn't mean they don't like you."

See what I mean? *No nonsense.* But I think it's a powerful message for the bashful ones afraid to step out of their own way. Leigh does tell creatives to keep their art as a hobby if they cannot get comfortable with putting it out there. Although listening to Leigh's tough love may be hard for you, stick with it (at least for the rest of this chapter).

Leigh has dealt with many creatives who lacked the confidence to pursue their dream. Heck, she admits to—at one time—*being* one of them. In 1998, she struggled with using her creativity in her every day life. (Note: She was a lawyer, totally on the opposite end of the right-brain function, but she knew how to integrate creativity into legal practice.) But that wasn't enough. Leigh knew that her purpose was to teach other women how to use their creativity to their full potential. That's why she left the field of law and created www.teras-wish.com, which, incidentally, is a great resource for those who want to get inspired. One of the road blocks the many women Leigh helped had was getting their work out there. Why? Because they feared rejection. So how can you have the guts to put your work out there? "Let go of your ego," suggests Leigh.

She uses a strong analogy relating to writing to illustrate her point. Leigh says that if you write, your work will be edited. "I have been blessed to work with wonderful editors that have improved my work," she says. "You have to view what you do as part of a team effort. You come up with the idea, but others will hone it so that it is marketable."

It's as if she's taken the fear of rejection and transformed the idea of it into one of constructive criticism. When you look at it that way, it doesn't seem too bad. After all, all creatives starting out want to improve; and most do realize they'll have to suck it up and listen to what may not be what they want to hear.

"Each of you have your own area of expertise," she says. "Yours is to create, theirs is to take your work and make it something someone will buy. If you are lucky, you will get someone who improves your work and makes your book or product a bestseller. See yourself as part of a team, and embrace those you work with that way."

Somehow, Leigh's outlook makes putting your work out there a little less frightening, don't you think? As time has gone on for me, I've also learned to take constructive criticism one step further. You don't have to agree with everything that everyone says, because when you think about it, it's just *one* person's opinion. Whenever I hear feedback I don't like, I take a step back and consider the source before I react.

If the source is someone I respect in their field, I try to see where they're coming from, and see if I can utilize their sometimes snide comments to improve my work. Sometimes, it's *just* an opinion, and there is nothing constructive about it. So what do I do with an opinion that's not constructive? Discard it!

I recently got a rejection about this book. The first thing I thought when I saw the e-mail from a person we'll call "Judge" wasn't that his opinion was rudely written and that he lacked the ability to give *polite* constructive criticism. As someone in the publishing industry, I wondered why he hadn't heeded the age-old advice of "choosing your words." Angered, I dismissed his claim.

But then I considered the source. Judge is well respected in the creative industry. He's been published many times. I've even read his work and liked it. I found value in it. So I listened to what he had to say and dissected where he was coming from. But I couldn't agree with him on his main point, which would have changed the identity of my book as a whole.

In the end, I think it's a matter of creativity in my case. But it illustrates a valuable point. We should listen to what others have to say about our work. Over time, it won't sting as much when we don't like what we hear. But in the beginning, it's a valuable step. It also taught me to evaluate my sources and give myself respect. Joe Schmoe on the street could disapprove of my book all he wanted with his *opinion*; at least I valued Judge's *constructive criticism* because of his industry background. So I chose to listen to the source in this case, and see what it had to say instead of being devastated. (Though panic is still sometimes my first reaction.)

In many cases during my writing career, the criticisms hurt a little at first, but it helped when I put my ego out of the way and listened to what the person had to say. In this case, you can see how I've grown to trust my instincts. Judge's advice was helpful, but I'm not bending.

"Sometimes you just get rejected because the person who saw it didn't like it. In that case, it is personal preference," says Leigh. Right on, sister.

Making Micromovements

In her book *Make Your Creative Dreams REAL*, author and artist Susan Ariel Rainbow Kennedy, known as SARK, describes the concept of micromovements. I consider these very useful for creatives who are shy about putting their work out in the public eye.

A micromovement, according to SARK, is designed especially for procrastinators and perfectionists (most of us fall into this category, don't we?). The concept is that with all of the creative ideas swirling around in our heads, it's best to focus on one thing at least for five minutes. If you get through five minutes and want to keep going—go! If not, continue another time; you may decide to scrap the project all together. That's okay. SARK gives us gentle permission to flow with our creativity. So if hounding down galleries to present your work seems overwhelming, start with one. Make *one* your goal for the day, and just see where it takes you.

SARK also says that recognizing a fear helps it lose power. Because many creatives fear putting their work out there for several reasons, she points out four different types of fears: anticipatory, irrational, catastrophizing and rational. An example of an anticipatory fear is saying "What if?" about something. ("What if the gallery doesn't like my painting?"), while an irrational fear would be that the owner of the gallery will take a glance at your work and throw you out of the gallery. Take it a step further and your fear is catastrophic: The gallery owner pushes you out the door. But some fears are rational, and worth exploring. If the gallery owner doesn't like your latest piece, you may fear that you will be so upset you won't create anymore.

That's when I say you have to *dissect* the fear, just as I dissected rejection above and broke it into opinion and constructive criticism. For example, do you really think *one* person will take *all* of your creative juice from you? Maybe for a few hours, or even days at the worst, but your passion will call you back. This is also when you have to evaluate whether you really want to live off your talents, or just pursue them it as a hobby. Either option is okay; but choose the one that suits you best.

When I received rejection at the beginning of my career, it would usually devastate me, sometimes for about an hour, sometimes for the rest of what would be come a somewhat bitter day. Eventually, I evaluated what I wanted to do. Knowing that writing was my passion, I decided to either ignore the criticism or take it into consideration (you'll learn more about this in Chapter 3, where we explore how to cope with and use rejection to your advantage).

The point is, putting your work out there *is* hard. But you have to do as Nike says and "Just Do It." That doesn't mean you can't take micromovements to get your work out there. *Research* galleries. *Talk* to other artists. *Look* at the kinds of work they carry. *Call* on your friends for support. These are valuable tools that you have in your creative toolbox to make taking the next step—or even a baby step—a little less daunting. Think of it as a micromovement and it's hardly a full step at all.

CREATIVE PROFILE
Tera Leigh
Author and Artist
Shawnee, Oklahoma

Getting Started
Tera Leigh is a former attorney who ran an Internet marketing firm, taught new media marketing for UCLA and Cal State–Long Beach Extension programs, and provided consulting on how to market women creators to some of the craft industry's largest manufacturers. In 1999, she signed her first book deal, co-licensed a product line and began to write for magazines. She also has an online radio show.

Growing a Thick Skin
Tera turns to Maya Angelou for wisdom about controlling what happens to us, saying that being thick skinned is a choice. If an artist puts there work out for display, they can find a way to be hurt by someone's reactions to it. "Choose to be a businessperson, believe in your product and if someone doesn't like what you do, move on until you find someone who does," she says.

When Business Is Slow
"Work full-time even if you don't have enough business," says Tera, who recommends creating art on spec, focusing on public relations or joining a networking group. "As an artist, usually 30 percent of my time is spent working on art or writing. The rest is administrative, public relations, marketing, etc."

For more information about Tera, visit www.teraleigh.com.

CHAPTER 3

✦

FACING REJECTION

Ask any creative person who has put their work out there, and they will tell you that rejection is imminent, and quite difficult to cope with, too. That's because writers and artists manufacture their own work. It comes from so deeply within that a rejected magazine article idea can feel like a slap in the face. And it's bound to happen; not everyone will like your work. What many freelancers grow to realize is that having your work rebuffed is standard. The artistic industry is subjective; an abstract piece of art may not make sense to one gallery, but may be easily comprehensible and appeal to another.

While I'd never consider my splattered spare-time canvasses to be gallery worthy, I do, as a writer, feel a wave of disappointment each time I scan the word "unfortunately" in a rejection letter. No matter what industry you're in, you're bound to run into no's when trying to sell yourself … or your stuff. At first, every rejection can be heart wrenching. I've mentally beaten myself up over more rejections than I care to admit.

Most seasoned creatives have learned to cope with negative responses over the years. It's imperative to note, however, that you don't just stop taking it personally. You don't even arrive at a place where rejection won't bother you, if you're like most creative types.

If you're lucky, you come to a sense of peace and acceptance, after endless rejection letters and self-induced pep talks. It is then, and only then, that a creatively self-employed worker will learn how to truly cope with, and learn from, rejection.

In this chapter, you'll learn what happens after you have the guts to put your work out there. You'll see how others deal with refusal, and hopefully feel better prepared to face the possibility of rejection.

∗   ∗   ∗

I would have to say that my worst wave of rejection came each time I repeatedly polished my first book and pitched it to agents and publishers. Each time I finally got it out there, I got a letter that began with the word "unfortunately." I had been rejected. Cast off. Rebuffed. And I sure as heck didn't get published. At first I stomped my feet and cried like a cranky toddler. *I put so much work into my bestseller-to-be. How could they possibly reject me?* I thought. To this day, I don't know. But I *did* learn more about the publishing industry during the process. With each letter, I got tips and ideas to help me better propose my idea.

Is that book published, you ask? Not *yet.* That leaves plenty of room for rejection, because I plan to pitch it again, someday. Inside, an abundance of impatience awaits me as I think about once again attempting the sale of my manuscript. (It was on the back burner while this project was in the works.) I have to admit; for as many times as the book got an "unfortunately," I still rebounded inside with hope. Sometimes it took a while to muster the optimism back up, but I always did. I persisted to make the proposal better. Send it to more agents. Push, push, push. I had to inject some hope into the rejection cycle that *is* book publishing. It took years of picking myself up, repairing my work and assembling the courage to put it back out there. So between resurgences of mass proposal sending, I got back up and was ready to face the world again. *They will take my book,* I told myself.

I got bites from agents, but I also got more rejection letters. (The book is a memoir, so I sometimes interpreted the rejections as the publisher saying that my life wasn't worth reading about. I'm still working to mentally replace that message with "This wasn't the right publisher for my baby.") I have to say, if it weren't for the rejection I wouldn't have pushed harder to make my manuscript something they wanted to see. I wouldn't have dared to spill more of myself onto the pages, or tried to learn as much about the publishing industry as I could.

Even though requests for the proposal were coming in, I grew exhausted. After years of waiting for an agent to bite, going back to rewrite the proposal, putting it out there again and repeating the process, I decided to focus on something new. Not caring whether the memoir ever really became reality, I felt more motivated to write about what I *knew* instead of what I had already experienced. Somehow, once I started letting myself grow from continued rejection, I was more willing to put my memoir to the side. You see, I knew the fear that came with leaving a steady job. I knew how hard it was to put myself out there. And when I did it, I stood regularly next to rejection. I knew about all of the toils that came with freelancing. And I knew that no one was talking about the ups and downs of creative living. So I scrapped the memoir idea for the time being and became fascinated with the process of creative self-employment.

And I was writing. Writing while my memoir proposals were out to agents. I didn't care if that book sold or not right away. I could write a book about what I *knew*—and I knew all about the fears and joys that came with self-employment. Better yet, I knew the ins and outs of *creative* self-employment. *It could be a book … A really good book. A meaningful book. A book that would appeal to a wider audience. A book that would make a difference,* I thought.

Now I had something to sell.

So I chose to put the idea for this book out there. I sent proposals to any address that would take them. After all, as someone who learned how to craft proposals by years of trial and error, I came up with the concept for this book pretty quickly, even easily. The reviews came back great—many agents wanted to see the manuscript and enjoyed it. This was a more general book that could attract a broader audience. They saw a huge market for it. My proposal had wooed them. Nothing could stop me now. I was destined to be taken on by a large New York publishing house with a book tour set out before me. The idea would be huge. It would be the first book of its kind. Truly revolutionary.

But after the agents reviewed it, the majority said they weren't "passionate enough" to sell this book. But oh yeah, they *loved* the concept, and the writing. So there I was again. I had the proposal down and a good know-how of the publishing industry. Killer idea. Polished. People were raving. *But it's still not good enough?*

That's when I got fed up and realized that if they weren't fervent enough about helping thousands upon thousands of people in this situation, which no one is really talking about publicly, then I would do it *myself*. Just like I launched my self-employed writing career. By myself. I would *self-publish* this book. *Voilà.*

So I guess there is a good aspect to the refusal cycle that comes with creative self-employment: *learning from our attempts.* Inject a little optimism into the mix, and don't forget to toss in persistence. My book, or books, never went where I expected them to. Heck, my memoir manuscript gets ripped to pieces about every six months. I have a resurgence of hope every now and then. But you know what? It's not that book's time yet. And I'm okay with that. I focused on this book and made it happen. Shortly before this book was published, an idea I submitted for a nonfiction book eons ago was accepted by a publisher. It will be my next venture.

People always ask me where I get my drive and how I stay motivated. They think I'm an eternal optimist who never gets run down. Not true whatsoever. So, what helps me stay focused? Rejection. Tears. Frustration.

This book did not come easily. I didn't always believe that there was good in denial. But after time—lots of it—I was able to emerge on the other end in a better place than I could have ever been. It was rejection that led me to write this book. It was rejection that made me stronger. Do I still get ticked off when an editor doesn't like something I write, or when I get a letter back from an agent saying that my memoir was "Lovely, but not right for us?" Of course I get upset. But I look to the past, and I learn from it. And what can I tell you about rejection? It takes time to accept it. Over and over again, until you can see past it and learn from it. Go beyond it. Do better.

So that's *my* story. Let's hear some others.

Out on a Limb

Allison Compton, founder of www.artespy.com, paints portraits and creates sculptures while she bounces back and forth among Illinois, Virginia, California and New York. For her, rejection is a paramount issue. She knows that people are opinionated, and negative responses are "a given." Yet when she went out on a limb and offered her portraits, usually $1,000, for $10 in a park just to get more experience and notoriety, she was amazed that people refused her solicitation. "I tried to treat it as a performance art or real-world drawing class for myself," says Compton, who hoped to improve her craft by mass-producing artwork.

As an artist, she realizes rejection also comes with not having her work accepted for gallery representation. This includes the inevitable, "Sorry, not for us" replies. "Everyone says to persevere, but it is hard," Compton says. "You must continue until someone says yes.

Believing in yourself and art is crucial." Sounds easy, but for many, it's not a piece of cake at first. Even veteran creatives experience insecurities.

"I'd rather receive a reaction because it means that the art got to the viewer. It's hard, especially when you're attacked in a critique with peers or ... read a negative review in the papers, but over time, with confidence and maturity, you stop caring about what others think because you have to true to yourself and God," Compton adds.

Compton faces another form of rejection. She has had issues with her family regarding her career. She says she comes from a family of artists who tried to deter her from following in their footsteps. Compton didn't want to disappoint her family by pursuing her dreams, but says she knew she had to listen to her heart. "In the end, I had to be true to myself," says Compton, who cast off her family's opinions and decided to chase her dreams. She says still struggles to make the rent some months, but wouldn't have it any other way.

Compton is a good example of a creative type who followed her dream in many ways and overcame rejection to do so. Getting clients can be difficult—and, she says, it also feels humiliating to have to try to appease others—but she also overcame refusal from her family and pressed on to achieve success. Though times were rough for her, it was her persistence that helped her prevail.

Falling Down, Standing Up

Celeste Heiter, a writer from California, agrees that persistence is key to thriving in the freelance world and combating rejection. And she's had her fair share of negative responses. For Heiter, breaking into a new market or creating a new client relationship can be difficult.

It sure is. Most creatives wonder if they're good enough, if their work is up to par and if potential clients will choose them. In the beginning, it's all about pleasing everyone, isn't it? You want to establish a client base, so you go off the deep end at times to satisfy clients. But after a while, and after many rejections, creatives can begin to see that a negative response is not the end of the world. In fact, you can decline potential clients when you have enough business built. It's just getting to that point that can be so hard. The path can be paved with refusal. But Heiter currently has many steady clients who she says are pleased with her work. She feels that her persistence is what counteracts the negative aspects that rejection can bring upon a creative freelancer.

"I am nothing if not persistent, and am always optimistic that someone somewhere will want what I have to offer," says Heiter, the author of seven books for ThingsAsian Press.

She says that living by the Japanese proverb, "Fall down seven times, stand up eight," has helped her persevere as a full-time freelance writer. And that's exactly what she does to get over any thoughts of rejection or failure that cross her mind.

For Heiter, it sounds easy. Truth be told, for many of us, it is not. The ups and downs of rejection and acceptance can feel like a roller coaster, and it's easy to feel nauseated after a while—or even to want to stop the ride completely.

Reasons for Rejection

Tamra Orr, a freelance writer from Oregon, offered a fresh, honest perspective when asked about how she deals with rejection. She says writers like her can't take it personally because editors see a lot coming across their desks and only know if what they see is what they need at the moment. "They don't know how much time, sweat and emotions you have invested," she offers.

But if you continually get rejected, she warns, it's time to re-evaluate what you're doing. Sometimes writers and artists do not investigate their target markets properly, or follow submission guidelines. That can have a huge impact on rejection, as many companies will not look at something that isn't in the right format or packaging. I think she speaks so honestly because she has been there and has gotten past getting bitter about rejection. Instead, she's used her bad experiences to evaluate what she can do to get her work approved the next time around. "The key is balancing your own passion for your work and realizing the reality of it in today's world. For this, you need the input from others and not just family members who love you."

Although it's nice to be coddled when you get one of those infamous rejection letters, it is also smart to look objectively at what you did or did not do to cause the reaction. From there, you can move on to a path where those letters are a thing of the past.

That's what works for Chris Tomlinson, a graphic designer based in Illinois. He says he deals with rejection on a monthly, if not weekly, basis. But he looks at it objectively after he has his initial reactions. "I handle rejection a bit poorly, but I never express that feeling in front of a customer/client. And I never show that side to friends, family or business associates," says Tomlinson, who worked as a police dispatcher before taking the creative plunge.

He says he goes through three steps of emotion when he gets rejected. First, he is upset. Then, he's downright angry. But finally, he gets focused. That's when he looks back to see where he may have failed. He looks at each situation as objectively as possible to determine why he wasn't chosen and how he can make his service better the next time around.

It's really all you can do. When creatives can cool down and examine the situation, they avoid built-up tension and needless anger.

Rebuffed and Stressed—But Still Published

Katrina Martin Davenport didn't face a whole lot of rejection whe the first publisher she queried picked up her first children's book *Denise's Mold*. It was a fabulous children's book, and Martin Daven port thought she hit gold when it was in print. "However, once i came time to try to sell the book, I was faced with all kinds of rejec tion," recalls Martin Davenport, a California-based children's boo author, photographer and tutor. "Bookstores were reluctant to se up events."

Martin Davenport struggled to get reviews, which would help t create a "buzz" for her book. Just about every aspect of marketin was placed on her, which she did not expect because she had a pub lisher. (Nowadays, most authors pick up a lot of the slack, eve when a commercial publisher accepts them.)

"It takes a lot of perseverance," says Martin Davenport, who stil comes face to face with rejection. "I do not deal well with rejection so it's been taking a toll on me. I feel stressed out. I feel like ther must be some magic formula that I can figure out that will lead t more book sales."

Even though Martin Davenport has sold a good number of cop ies of *Denise's Mold*, she admits that she had a larger number i mind. "Since I haven't met that, I have a feeling of failure," she says "Baby steps and small goals are better. That's what I'm working o right now. That, and putting my butt in my chair to write." That' right, Martin Davenport is working on more books. But she als feels frustrated being an author because she has to do so much wor to sell her book and promote herself.

"But that's the reality, and I'm trying to work within thos parameters," says Martin Davenport. And there's an upside to th creative life for this author in her late 20s. At the end of the day, sh followed a dream, wrote a book and even published it. She's a author, high books sales or not.

In 2005, Martin Davenport dropped the publisher, but is still pursuing sales and continues writing. She plans to publish again, perhaps even by herself. For her, rejection wasn't outright (after all, she *did* get published!), but the entire situation left her feeling let down. Months later, she still struggles to find her place as a writer. But one thing about Martin Davenport that is notable is her persistence to keep writing. You have to figure that if she was published before, it's likely to happen again.

Be a Rejection Collector

Did you say rejection *collector*? Yep. Our next creative has an interesting take on accepting rejection, one that, once you listen to her perspective makes good sense. Adriana Diaz, a life coach from California, believes there are five keys to surviving the rejection inherent in the artist's life: understanding, attitude, pragmatism, perseverance and resilience. She not only coaches people living creative lives through Creative Life Coaching, but is a writer, artist and educator. She's juried exhibitions, conducted casting for theater and written *Freeing the Creative Spirit, Drawing on the Power of Art to Tap the Magic and Wisdom Within.*

"As a young artist, every rejection brought a flood of self-recrimination and tough critique of my work. I presumed, as many do, that the rejection of the work meant that the work was 'not good enough,'" she says. "Now I know that work is not actually rejected at all, it is simply not chosen."

She says if work is rejected, it does not mean you are a failure. "Your work just did not meet the taste of the juror, or didn't fit into the specific situation," she explains. "It's important to realize that in curating or selecting creative work, the juror has to consider the overall flow and balance of the entire exhibition. So some work may not be selected because it doesn't quite fit with the combined harmony or rhythm of the exhibition being mounted."

It's never easy to have work come back unaccepted, Diaz says. "Everyone seeks praise, and fantasizes about 'being discovered' as one of the great creative geniuses of their century. In reality, however, art and publication systems are based on the rejection process." That's the key to overcoming rejection—once you see that you're not a failure and your work just didn't meet the standards or taste of *one* person, it's easier to accept and move on, and even learn from the experience.

Diaz says that the best attitude to have when it comes to rejection is to consider yourself a collector of rejections. Creative types can have their own evaluative process to grade the quality of each rejection received. So, if you want to know why your work was rejected, it's possible to inquire about that. But first be certain that you are ready to hear tough criticism if it comes your way.

"Having a collection of rejection notices and letters makes you a real artist. The longer you've been working, the more rejections you should have," she says. She once received a rejection letter from a publisher that was so glowing, she held on to it to reread on days she gets down. For Diaz, when the major publishing house told her what she sent was "very well-written," it hardly mattered that they didn't think enough people would read a book on that topic. "Well-written" is the phrase you highlight and hold in your heart, because that is the acknowledgement of your craft, Diaz says.

When I heard about Diaz's notion, the vengeful side of me came through at the thought of all the rejections I have collected. Not only would it be neat to gather rejections and learn from them, but who says you can't keep the letters and have a mass bonfire each time you collect a certain number of letters? Better yet, why not write a rejection letter back (but not send it)? Or you can just keep your rejection letters in a neat binder. My ideas may seem a little aggressive, but if you are one to anger easily, this may be a great release. No matter what you do, there is a plus to rejection—you just have to think creatively about how to deal with it.

The Boundary Between Work and Self

Ilise Benun, author and founder of Marketing Mentor, notes that rejection is both subjective and relative.

"What most often happens when we initially reach out or put our work out into the world is nothing. We get silence, no response. People don't call back or respond to e-mail messages, especially from people they've never heard of before," says the New Jersey consultant. "That is not to be confused with rejection, which is when someone says, 'No, thank you, this is not for me.' And they usually do it very politely, not with the aggression that most creatives imagine."

She says it is essential for creatives to separate their work from themselves, because a negative response regarding their work is *not* a rejection of themselves. Still, as creatives, we *put ourselves* into our work, so it's hard to remember to separate the two. "Creative people must learn to accept that most of the efforts they make will be in vain, but you must go through that process to find the perfect fits," she notes. "And they [creatives] can even be grateful for the rejection because it means they can move on to prospects that will be more open and interested."

Now *that's* creative thinking. She's rationalized what rejection means into a very simple truth: If you get rejected, it's not *you*—it simply means the work doesn't fit the outlet you wanted to place it in.

Another fine point she makes is that silence does not imply rejection. I would say about 70 percent of the queries I put out as a writer (most of them just pass along my resume and state that I'm here if the company needs freelance help) go unanswered. When I have gotten letters with "not at this time" or the ever-popular "unfortunately," it has been people writing back to tell me they cannot use my services. Over time, a thicker skin has built up because I take time to rationalize the disapprovals instead of just reacting. Then I can *process* what's happening during the creative process.

Boy, that's a lot of processing! But it works, sort of like cognitive-behavioral therapy for the creative mind: *Think* about things; don't just *react*. (A reaction is okay. Sometimes you need to scream or, say, take a mid-day swim in the ocean to cool off. And hey, you *can*! That's okay!)

Benun, a fellow self-employed woman, says that although people are not born with thick skin, they can acquire it over time. But she's careful to point out that most creatives do not take enough risks to get the practice necessary to develop a bulky skin, and therefore conclude that getting a thicker skin is not possible, or isn't their "style."

"As a result, they are unaccustomed to responses that can be interpreted negatively," she says. I like the way this gal thinks. She's all about taking risks by putting your work out there, facing rejection, but developing enough strength inside to cope with it and *not* go insane.

Building Confidence

As many creatives found out after taking the plunge into self-employment, confidence is not a given. It's earned. Or at least you stumble onto it. But it doesn't just arrive.

It can come in the feeling of *selling* a piece of art more so than in actually creating it—usually by the time you've decided to go into self-employment, you have enough acceptance of your craft. Confidence grows with growing to admire your own talents and your ability to thrive in business. So you're getting confident first by creating work that you are proud of, and then by being successful with it—in this case, selling the work. But becoming truly successful, including financially, comes from real assurance. And one moment of glory will not do it for you, I'm afraid. I think it happens over time, as we celebrate little victories.

It also happens when we realize that we're not alone. That's kind of the point of this entire book; for you to hear these stories and identify with them. Somehow, knowing you're not alone is a huge comfort—one that I think can combat the negatives associated with creative self-employment.

Getting a Second Opinion

Sometimes the support necessary to build self-assurance comes from reaching out to others. Erin Flynn, a writer and publicist from New York who founded Flynn Media in 2001, says she doubts her ability from time to time. So she sends some of her work to her brother, mother, or boyfriend to get a second opinion. Once she's confident in the piece, she submits it to the editor.

She's also a huge fan of building up professional support to gain and build up confidence. She recommends that creatives join a networking group, such as a chamber of commerce. "Attend regular meetings and you will develop relationships with other businesspeople. Bounce issues off of them if you're not sure what to do; no doubt you will become friends with some members of the group," Flynn says. "And it doesn't hurt for a large group of professionals to know what you do so they can refer business your way."

From her advice, it's clear to see that Flynn's self-reliance comes from reaching out to others. Though it can be harder, one can also build it up in time by believing in themselves. (We'll discuss that in Chapter 4.) But sometimes that seems so hard to do.

So, how exactly *do* you build confidence?

Developing "Rejection Resilience"

In her book *The 12 Secrets of Highly Creative Women*, Gail McMeekin introduces the concept of "rejection resilience." As the term implies, rejection resilience is the ability to bounce back from rejection. For many, it does not happen easily, but luckily it will happen eventually if you nurture your creative spirit for success. Like many processes discussed in this book, rejection resilience develops over time.

"We must be able to move in the world knowing that not everyone will approve of us or our creative accomplishments consistently," McMeekin writes in her book. Developing rejection resilience, she explains, means "learning to prop ourselves up." Even McMeekin knows that perseverance is vital. She advises doing a psychological check on yourself to see how prepared you are to face rejection, and says that most people need a support system to depend on when they encounter negativity and disappointment. In addition, it's important to assess personal vulnerabilities so you are aware of them, she says. Once that's done, you can see where you need to support yourself.

In Martin Davenport's case (remember her from the section "Rebuffed and Stressed—But Still Published?"), she was vulnerable to feelings of failure with her book sales, though she had accomplished the task of getting *Denise's Mold* published. For her, knowing that her book sales were upsetting meant she had to realize that it was going to be difficult to increase them. But by accepting her "parameters," she has moved herself into a more self-supporting mindset.

You may be wondering if I have any suggestions for building confidence. Honestly, I don't believe there is any one way to build self-reliance that will work for all of us. You have to be good at what you do, and put yourself out there to prove that others agree. In my case, I ventured out into various industries to write materials for a wide variety of companies. I found that even when I was writing on a topic I did not know much about, I did well. I knew I could write, and by expanding my horizons, I gave my clients the chance to approve of me. In just about every case, they have. I've learned not to rely on their approval to know I'm good, but it helps to have some endorsements.

Still up for more advice to create confidence in your work? Good—there are plenty more strategies I've got to share with you!

A Little More Personal

Sharon Good, a life coach from New York City, agrees that coping with rejection is not easy for self-employed creative types. As someone who consults with creatively self-employed writers, designers and artists, Good knows that facing the feelings that come with rejection, and dealing with them in a healthy way, is important.

"First, separate yourself from your work," Good advises. "Creative work is very personal, so this can be hard to do." She says it is important to be as objective as you can and understand that people have all kinds of opinions. When faced with rejection, look at what the rejecter says and evaluate it for yourself. Do you agree with what the person said? Is there anything there that would improve your work? Do you have a unique style that people don't "get" and haven't found your audience yet? These are all helpful questions freelancers should ask themselves to see if the comment is worth getting upset about. And if it is, you do not have to get upset. You can *learn* from the criticism and use it to better your work.

"Second, you have to build up a tough skin," Good says. "When you're putting yourself out there, becoming more visible, people feel a right to criticize. They're not always gentle, and even when they are, it can hurt." I think the key here is to step back and process rejection. Choose how you want to react, instead of letting your emotions take over. The more you take this "break" to decide how you want to feel, the more automatic it will become. I think in the long run, you'll appreciate having this quality (as will your clients).

As a young actress, Good remembers receiving rejections that were sometimes devastating. "I would give myself time to heal, continue working on my craft, and when I was ready, put myself out there again." Gradually, the amount of time between rejection and getting out again got shorter and shorter. "Unless you want to create just for yourself, you have to take the risk of being visible and facing rejection or criticism," she says.

That's why a support system is Good's third tip. Having people who believe in you to support you when you're down helps soften a blow. (This, by the way, is completely natural, even for a seasoned creative.)

"If someone sends you positive feedback, keep it," advises Good. "Start a file that you can look at when you're feeling discouraged. Have people who are willing to let you call and vent when you've faced a tough rejection."

Having faith in yourself, your work and your creative vision does not come overnight, but Good says knowing that is also important. I have to agree. There's a reason why you stepped into your career. If you've been getting work in the past, there's obviously talent that more people can benefit from. A little criticism and rejection is bound to happen; pretending that it won't will only make it harder to accept when it does happen. Let it. Learn to cope with the down times so you don't go down with them each time they happen.

"You may be a work in progress, but your vision is your own, and you have a right to shape it however you want. Keep your eye on your target, and do not let anyone talk you out of it," she says.

"If Barbra Streisand had had a nose job and tried to fit into the 'normal' mold, she wouldn't be the superstar she is today."

∗   ∗   ∗

Von Glitschka, a graphic designer and illustrator from Oregon, compares his work to that of others in his field. "Sometimes, seeing their excellent work is so intimidating that I entertain the thought of giving up," he confesses. "I think that's the highest compliment you can give an artist—telling them that their work makes you want to quit."

Yes, he takes art so personally that he compares himself to other people. Most of us do. When it doesn't turn into a self-esteem douser, this habit can inspire us to do better. When it comes to rejection, Glitschka says comparing himself to others can bum him out. "Then it turns to motivation to improve and do better," he says. "I guess I view failure as a second chance with the added benefit of knowing what doesn't work, so it's limiting the risk the second time around. Fail more than once, then you have that much more chance of succeeding."

This is the type of healthy attitude that will miraculously make rejection feel less potent. The key is practicing. Changing your attitude. Taking up a new behavior. Because it's just too easy to fall into a self-defeating slump.

Using Support to Combat Refusal

As Good said, *support*—whether from others or from creating an inner voice of strength (both are best if you ask me)—is essential for self-employed creatives because rejection is a part of the job that you can't avoid. *Support* is the secret ingredient you toss in that no one can see, and it makes all the difference.

Regrettably, letters with the inevitable "unfortunately" in them will come along. Submissions will be rebuffed. Freelancers will lose clients. But it's the awareness to strengthen oneself, and to practice persistence, that will turn rejection into something to learn from—something that can, in fact, help you improve your craft. No matter how you gain confidence, you can rest assured that with the power of time, it will come.

10 TOOLS FOR DEALING WITH CRITICISM AND REJECTION

1. Be Open. You may be hoping for a specific reaction or response to your work, or a specific result of an audition, gallery submission, performance or contest entry. If you've done your best and you're rejected or criticized, you might feel that you've "failed," and it's probably hard to see anything positive about the situation. Try to be open to the possibility that this "failure" is actually leading you to something else, usually something better than what you thought you wanted. As I read once in Cheryl Richardson's newsletter, "Any rejection is God's protection."

2. Be Consistent. Keep going, doing the little things every day that keep you creative and that keep you connected to other artists and to your customers. The dramatic moments and big wins and losses will come and go. Have a steady routine you can keep coming back to, and this will help to place any criticism or rejection into perspective. Today is a new day, another day you get to be an artist.

3. Be Focused. Keep your goal in mind, and always be mindful of why you're doing what you're doing. That will help you focus on the big picture and not get tripped up by each bump in the road along the way.

4. Be Resilient. Remember that your sense of self-worth comes from inside of you. When you're able to be confident in yourself regardless of the feedback you get from external sources, you're able to bounce back much more easily from any negative feedback that you may get.

5. Be Positive. Focus your attention on the positive and you'll attract more of it. This is the premise of the "law of attraction," and I've certainly seen it work in my own life. Hear the positive feedback you receive and replay it over in your mind whenever you need to.

Continued on next page.

10 TOOLS FOR DEALING WITH CRITICISM AND REJECTION

6. Be Clear. Approach constructive feedback with an accurate perspective, not muddled with thoughts from your own inner critic. Take it as a helpful tool for your own growth, and remember that ultimately the only opinion that matters is your own—because you need to be happy with what you're producing.

7. Be Grateful. Be gracious to your critics, accept all of the feedback you receive, sit quietly and let it sink in. Be grateful to be actively creating, to have gotten past the fear and other roadblocks. Be grateful for the opportunity to have your work seen and heard. Some never get the chance.

8. Be Responsive. Decide consciously what to do with feedback before responding, instead of reacting with the first thought or words that come to mind.

9. Be Selective. Once you've decided what to do the feedback you've received, be selective and willing to let go of the hurtful feedback. This usually doesn't have anything to do with you anyway; it's a reflection of that person's own happiness, state of mind and comfort with themselves.

10. Be Loving. Be loving of your [inner] critic and *especially* of yourself. Plan some self-care treats for the day of the audition or submission. Regardless of the outcome, you deserve it!

Tips provided by Linda Dessau of www.genuinecoaching.com.

CREATIVE PROFILE
Erin Flynn
Publicist and Writer
Philadelphia, Pennsylvania

Getting Started

Before founding Flynn Media in 2001, Erin Flynn worked for an international sales training company as a writer and editor. Her primary role there was to customize hundreds of training programs each year for Fortune 500 clients in every field.

Avoiding Stress When Business Gets Slow

"I think it's just a matter of plugging away, keeping a positive attitude and not getting discouraged when you have slow months," says Erin. "I've grown to enjoy the sales work—when I close a deal and the client does not balk at my price, it's one of the best feelings in the world. I've become more confident as a result of being self-employed. But it can be very scary at first."

Resisting Rejection

"With any creative field, there is going to be rejection," Erin notes. "Some people love my writing style; other clients haven't been so thrilled. But you have to risk the rejection in order to succeed."

For more information about Erin, visit www.flynnmedia.com.

CHAPTER 4

◆

TRUST YOURSELF

Sometimes I feel like Dr. Emmett Brown, or the "Doc," in the *Back to the Future* movies. Like the scattered genius, I'm brimming with new businesses to target for copywriting, and even more publishing ideas. Some of these thoughts, like this book, actually made it to the write-down phase, while other aspirations remain locked in my mind and may never come to fruition simply because there's a lot floating around upstairs. For other writers like me, a spare notebook with scribbles holds valuable ideas, all spewing from some unknown energy inside. I say it's how the creative mind works.

The frenzy in my mind really took off when I became a freelance writer. Not only were my creative endeavors fun to dream up, but without the security of a corporate job, I'd have to churn something out to make a living. And so I was flooded with ideas, thinking about magazine writing, editing and copywriting, all the while yearning to be an author as well. With all the ambition came hope. With optimism came motivation. With enthusiasm came proposals and query letters. And like every writer who attempts to get published, I got rejected. Every creative knows what that can feel like.

When I began to explore the ups and downs I faced personally, otherwise known as the incubation period for this book, I started to think up ways that I could fight the discouraging feelings that came with negative responses. That's when another series of ups and downs came along for me. Not only were there physical rejection letters (and accomplishments along the way), but there was now a bipolar aspect that went along with my moods each time something good or bad happened. I was letting the opinions of other people shift my moods. And as they say, no one can put you down unless you let them. I was letting them.

When something good happened, such as a client loving my work and giving me more, I was elated. But when a downer swept over, such as a magazine article getting cast off, I let it deflate me. This happened over and over, multiple times a day. It is a bad example of going with the flow. There was no balance during this time in my life, because everyone else dictated how I felt. And when I wasn't feeling my best, business would suffer. Still being in my mid-20s at the time, and much like a child, I cried, "Unfair!"

Living as if life is carrying you along in the current can be both bad and good. It can be good to go with the flow, which relieves the urge to control everything and live perfectly. For me, I found that my thin skin left me vulnerable to every negative response out there, so I wasn't going with the flow, I was getting washed over by it. When I crashed, I crashed hard mentally. And that started letting voices of doubt and fear creep in. How could this be? I was living my dream career—it was all supposed to be peachy. I knew it would not be perfect. I knew rejection would find me. I just didn't expect it to slap me across the face. But was it really hitting me that hard? Or was I the one at fault for letting it?

Starting out, even the toughest creative types have to learn—by the trial and error—to go with the flow, yet not let the wave overtake them. Knowing that there is a balance out there that must be achieved to feel secure, many creatively self-employed people learn that this can be done only by building up inner strength and trust-

ing in themselves. A writer would need to know that no one is goin
to drag him or her out of bed to finish a magazine article. And n
one's going to tell him or her that "everything's going to be okay,"
the piece gets rejected.

The truth is, in an industry where you're told to b
thick-skinned, some of us are not. But we do have other tools t
help us get by, to build ourselves up and be able, eventually, to rid
a wave. Better yet, it's possible to enjoy the waves rushing over ou
faces as we cruise safely to shore.

That's why this chapter is separate from the previous one wher
we discussed dealing with rejection and building confidence. As yo
remember, I mentioned letting time mold you. Heal you. Build yo
up. Because success comes with time and in this industry you hav
to learn by trial and error. In many cases, you can beat the odds jus
by hanging on. And if you can learn a few tricks to trust yourself
little more, you can really do well!

But simply letting time pass isn't good enough. While you ca
employ strategies and tactics to boost your confidence, you can als
build yourself up *by* yourself. How? *Trust* yourself.

Confidence Doesn't Come Easily, But It *Will* Come

Although there are down sides to her career, Lara McGlashan woul
not have it any other way. She's always been self-employed in som
way or another, except for a stint as a waitress. Now, the Californi
creative writes health and fitness articles, and has done so for si
years.

She has evolved into a self-assured writer over time, mostl
because she loves her work. She hasn't let fears over not havin
health care coverage, for example, cloud her assurance. "Sometimes
when I have to pay my health insurance every month, I think
might like to have a regular job. But then I go to the beach for a

hour in the middle of the day—because I can—and that thought flies out the window," says McGlashan.

What's so evolved about hearing her voice her opinions on creative self-employment is the maturity and ease in her statements. While some of us start out fretting about not working 9-to-5, for example, McGlashan has achieved a state of comfort and security with herself that comes only as creatives go through the trials and errors in their first few months and years of independent working.

For example, she has honed her best work practices, knowing that she is a procrastinator and works best "under the gun." And she's okay with that. "I work when I feel like working: weekends, mornings, nights … whenever. Writing is not something I can do on a 'have-to' basis," she says. "Creativity never comes on demand like cable programming." What words of wisdom! *Creative* words of wisdom, to boot!

So you're probably wondering how she makes it look so easy. The key is trusting yourself. And as I've noted, you don't just get there. You have to learn along the way. Luckily for you, creative self-employment is a fabulous teacher.

Facing the Fear of Freelancing

Designer Tamar Wallace, whom we met in Chapter 1, found it hard to adjust when she became self-employed. "Ironically, for me, the hardest thing about being self-employed is also the reason I chose to become self-employed: not having to answer to anyone else, and being my own boss," she says. "While this does allow for tremendous freedom, it also requires much more focus and self-discipline, something I didn't quite realize when I first became self-employed."

Although she loved being her own boss, the financial uncertainties and unstructured work time was something to get used to. Wallace says she missed punching out at 5 p.m. and being done with her job, and knew as a freelancer it would be more of a 24/7 job. "It was absolutely terrifying and exhilarating at the same time," she recalls.

That's because she was now in charge of all aspects of her income, from figuring out how much to charge, to making sure she got paid, to billing clients and reporting taxes—and oh yeah, designing. "If I knew then what I know now, I'm not sure I would have gone out on my own. However, I remember just feeling so elated the first few days of working for myself … I felt like I was finally doing what I was meant to do," says Wallace, who says that she envisioned working for herself since her childhood.

Another difficulty lies in work flow, and her ability to cope with slow times. She says she has often felt guilty for not being in the corporate 9-to-5 world, especially when business has been slow. When the finances are resting solely on her husband's income, Wallace says it can be complicated to trust in her work and the creative process.

"The guilt factor has increased tremendously since we had a child, because no matter how important my career is to me, my family comes first," says Wallace. She says that if she had to go back to 9-to-5 work, she would to do what's best for her family. She trusts that what she is doing now is what she should be doing, and knows that whatever situation comes up, she'll make her career work.

Stepping Up to the Challenge

"You'll never be a writer," Jennifer Hollowell's high school English teacher told her more than 10 years ago. Despite the injustice done by that educator, Hollowell used the negative, inappropriate comment to propel herself further. And wouldn't you know it, Hollowell is now a writer and artist with her own online studio and gallery.

"[That comment] stuck with me for a long time," says the Maine-based artist and wordsmith. Prior to self-employment, she worked at a bookstore, and was writing for small publications and newsletters for a few years. It was then that she started considering a writing career. "I found myself writing more and wanted to do this all the time—it had always been a part of me, but I didn't realize how strong," says Hollowell, who decided to take a leap of faith in 1999 when she became pregnant with her first son. She went full-time as a freelance writer, and also offered publicity services for self-published authors. Her talents came naturally, but the rise to success has come with some difficulties along the way.

Hollowell, still writing, remembers the odds she had to combat to make her career reality. Though support from others came and went (but never really stayed), Hollowell says she learned to rely on herself most of all. And that's the essence of this chapter. Support comes and goes. Confidence-builders fade. In the end, it's only *you*. You need to learn to rely on yourself if you want to succeed as a self-employed creative.

For Hollowell, daily self-assurance was necessary to help her trust herself and make her business flourish. She also read encouraging books, and relied heavily on *Simple Abundance* by Sarah Ban Breathnach and *The Artist's Way* by Julia Cameron. They helped her stay inspired and aided her in daily writing on a personal level, aside from her professional obligations. "No one else in my face-to-face life believed I could make this work," says Hollowell, now a mother of two. "I set out not only to prove to them that I could, but to also to prove it to myself. It almost felt like I was trying to prove to everyone that this really was my career. That was a huge motivational force."

What I like most about Hollowell is her proactive nature. She recited affirmations, read books and probably repeated mantras along with a slew of other otherwise out-of-the-box things to do. But they helped. She realized that she needed to build trust and confidence in herself, and she did it.

So did freelance writer Tamra Orr, whom we met in Chapter 3. One thing that has helped her have confidence in her abilities is to appreciate her own work. And if you can't yet appreciate it, draw upon others to give you feedback.

She brings up a valid insight—the value of getting objective constructive criticism from others in the industry. Once you can hone your skills enough to get nods from others in the field, self-reliance will also emerge. But you've got to have a tough skin, and if you don't, you'll automatically build one after learning to use constructive criticism to your advantage.

"I don't think any of us have thicker skin than the next one; it is the strength of our inner self esteem and confidence that varies from person to person and that is based on parenting, personality, etc.," says Orr, who jokes, "Just going into this kind of business will either make you thicker skinned or kill you off, one of the two."

She may be partly kidding, but when it comes down to it, she's right. You've got to get past rejection and develop self-assurance about your work and your potential to get ahead. And by now you know that this only happens through trial and error. We choose if we succeed or fail.

Orr says that if creatives adopt the right attitude about negative responses, it will help ease the blow should their work get rejected. For example, when an article she's written gets a "No," she knows that it didn't meet the editor's needs at that particular time. For writers, she warns them to follow the rules when it comes to reading writer's guidelines and submitting proper queries.

Once you're playing in the big leagues, it's important to make sure you're doing your very best to put in a good game. It's a lot easier to accept rejection if you know you have given it your all. And on the contrary, you'll build trust in yourself more easily when you know you've taken the job seriously and put your best foot forward.

Orr has taken an effort to not only avoid rejection, but to admire her own work. Sometimes that alone takes work. But it helps.

Katrina Martin Davenport, an author, photographer and tutor featured in the previous chapter, says building up a thick skin is key. Not only to battling rejection, but also to trusting yourself. "You can do this by realizing that your worth as a person is not tied up in how many gigs you get or whether or not your photos were published on the cover of a magazine. You have to find your worth inside yourself or you will never be able to enjoy your work, even if you are following your bliss," she says.

Take it from someone who has a lot of confidence and trust in herself and her work. Christine Miller, an artist and writer from California, has a simple philosophy for dealing with rejection and having faith in herself.

"I have to do the very best work I can do, put forth my best effort to get it seen, exhibited, published and sold, but beyond that I have to let go," says Miller. "Whatever I do, if it does not succeed, I cannot take that personally. It is not possible for me to discern in perfect detail what the public wants, and it would be foolish of me to try to squeeze my creative energy into someone else's idea of art or creative talent."

Wow. Sounds so simple, but for many of us, it can take years—even decades—to get to that point.

"I know I have talent," Miller continues. "How I use that talent to express myself may or may not be accepted or appreciated by the rest of the world. That is not up to me. All I can do is get my work out there and see what happens. If people respond to one thing but not another, I will keep on building what is giving me the best responses, and see where that takes me. As long as I can be authentic in my work, I will follow those leads as far as they can go."

Craving a positive attitude like that one? Let's help you build it! As creatives, we can be proactive and make attempts to build our confidence and thick skin, whether it be by reading books on the topic or leaning on a support system. Remember to use yourself as a tool, too. The mind can be very powerful when you make the conscious effort to turn down the volume on negative, self-defeating inner voices. Give yourself the advice you would give a friend, even if it feels unnatural. Over time, I think you'll take that advice and see things on a more positive note.

Trusting Yourself

So how do you get to a place were you can be your own cheerleader, or at least get on the right path to trusting yourself more? M.J. Ryan can help. She wrote an entire book on how to develop self-trust, and its principles can be applied directly to self-employed creatives. Heck, she's a creative type, too, so she has been through hard times and is living proof that you can succeed and thrive in this business.

Ryan has not only written eight books; the consultant serves as a coach to individuals and companies. Needless to say, her advice is quite valuable, and I found her book, *Trusting Yourself: How to Stop Feeling Overwhelmed and Live More Happily with Less Effort* to be a great comfort during my own down times. Ryan says many creative types panic when they hit a down time. Why?

"We've mystified the creative process," says Ryan, who lives in California and founded an independent publishing company in 1987. She points out that many creative people do not understand that there are ebbs and flows to the creative course. When artists and writers go through a down cycle, they feel empty and can think that is the end. Or that they're not good enough. Or that it's time to run back to corporate safety.

Not so, Ryan says. She doesn't offer a step-by-step plan for gaining self-trust, but does say that the best way to build it up is to play on past successes. If you're starting out as a graphic artist and have not a client in sight, for example, think about the successful student art show where you exhibited your work during college. Any success, even one unrelated to your field, can be used to motivate. Once you're motivated, you can put yourself out there a little. Will rejection come? Sure. But as Ryan emphasizes, it's part of the *process.*

Confidence and trust in oneself will naturally build as success is tasted, says Ryan. And the successes do not have to include a book publishing deal or an exhibit at a swanky gallery. Start small. Once you've done something and been successful at it, apply that mentality of "I've done it before, I can do it again" to an even bigger aspiration or project.

Ryan turns simple tips into thought-based journeys in her books, and for her clients. Instead of giving the strategies, she says she believes that the answers are inside all of us. When we get "stuck" (or down), we are simply disconnected from our resources. The answer to building self-trust? Keep going. Learn by trial and error, says Ryan. She knows all about voices of self-doubt, and calls them the "demons of the creative." But when they strike, Ryan says, "Just walk past them."

And here I was thinking it was best to tell them off.

Awareness and Acceptance Yield Self-Reliance

Using positive self-talk works to bid farewell to the "demons of the creative," but Ryan incorporates another concept into self-trust growth development. "The creative process is a right-brained activity," explains Ryan. This means that a self-employed crafter may be good at producing textiles, but when it comes to the business he or she needs to make it a success, but the left brain can get in the way. The left brain is good at company-related functions, such as discriminating, seeing things objectively and criticizing. Thus, the crafter may have problems interacting with clients, or marketing him- or herself. Panic and doubt can ensue, but it is not the creative's fault, Ryan says. The crafter is simply more gifted in using the right side of his or her brain.

So what should you do when you have the products but lack some business know-how to sell your services and material objects? "We all need to come to self-awareness," says Ryan. That means accepting what you're good or bad at. Knowing your strengths and weaknesses, you can move to self-acceptance. For example, the crafter needs to be aware that he or she may be better at sewing, but may not be as sharp at the selling his or her handbags. Luckily, others can help out by offering support or marketing help, and business skills can be learned. You'll hear more about this in Chapter 9.

Instead of hampering yourself by wondering, "What am I doing wrong?" Ryan suggests noticing what you do *well*. Accepting that you may need help with sales or marketing, for example, means that you need to seek out that help. There are plenty of books and business tips out there to help balance out the creative right-sided brain with left-brain practicality.

No Perfect Formula

When I set out to write this book, I knew I didn't want it to be a how-to publication. I wanted to simply put real voices out there, because I believe there is comfort where honesty and courage flourish. Ryan echoes my belief that there is no right way to succeed in your endeavor; creative self-employed success comes in accepting what each of us does best, and simply doing it.

Here's a more personal example. Coming straight out of 9-to-5-ville, I was astonished on days when I didn't have an assignment. If it was a Wednesday, I thought I had to be working. What happened on those weekdays when I twiddled my thumbs and sat at Starbucks? I was terrified. Quite literally. For me, it always seemed to be that there was a pressing deadline on a weekend, which was when I wanted to go kayaking, catch up on sleep or spend time with friends and family. Feeling guilty for sipping lattes on the Wednesday, I inflicted guilt on myself for not having regular-business-hours work. And then I worked all day Saturday to "make up for it." By the time Monday would roll around, I'd be pumped to work, but panic around 11 a.m. when I had ripped through my day's tasks. Uh-oh. Vicious, vicious cycle. You know what happens next. Actually, sometimes it still does.

I find that it takes a lot of positive self-talk, coupled with time (my best teacher) to build trust in myself. I have to believe that if I'm not busy one day, I'll be full of activity the next day—or in some cases, the next week. Over time, I've learned that this belief is okay. It's when I let go a little bit and trust the creative process, including creative voids (and even famines!), that the work comes in. As the cycle goes, I have weeks when I wish I could only work eight hours a day, and bust out 12-hour powerhouses to get it all done. Then there are void days. But I've learned to use them to relax. I've learned to trust that those are the days I'm meant to unwind.

That's just how it goes.

There is no perfect formula. I know that things will ebb and flow, and I learn by doing. Luckily, the panic doesn't creep up as much, because I'm getting the hang of this thing called the creative life. And before anyone jumps in, as Ryan says, they should be aware that it's a *process,* not a destination.

I think that just knowing this takes so much of the pressure off. It's okay to feel crummy at times. It's part of the process. Things will get better. I spent so many times worrying if things would be okay and then watching them come through. Eventually I got exhausted weighing myself down with worry, and just sort of stopped. I am more aware now that if a low comes, I simply need to hang on and let time pass until the good times come around again. Knowing this also enables me to have more balance when life spins sometimes out of control.

Life's an Experiment

With no clear how-to formula to offer, Ryan says the process of finding what things work for each of us is the beauty of creative, authentic living. "Rather than being helped to understand how *we* best function, how to find the solutions that work best for *us*, we have become people who look to others to define who we should be, how we should feel and how we should live," Ryan says in *Trusting Yourself.*

Think about it; how "authentic" are the authentic lives we've chosen to lead if we follow the path of others? It's more fun to create our own paths, don't you think?

*   *   *

I invite you to give yourself permission to trust yourself. Trust the process. Put it to the test. Do your best and watch the success come back to you. Pretend you're confident and self-trusting—even if you feel anything but! Imagine success. See it. Taste it. Soon enough, you'll see that you got yourself there.

CREATIVE PROFILE
M.J. Ryan
Author, Consultant
Walnut Creek, California

Getting Started
M.J. Ryan began editing as soon as she got out of college. Though she did some writing at a weekly newspaper, she used her editing talents and got into magazines. In 1987, she founded Conari Press as an independent publisher and served as CEO. To fund the company, she started ghostwriting books. About 10 years ago, she started publishing books.

Hardships That Exist
"For me, personally, there's no one to guarantee a paycheck," says M.J.

A Mission in Life
M.J. wanted so badly to help others that she's used her gift of writing to publish eight books, though she admits that writing comes easily to her and she wants to use it beyond getting published. "I feel like my mission in life is to uncover [other people's] gifts and talents," says M.J., who now also works as a consultant with Professional Thinking Partners. She is a speaker and workshop leader on how to cultivate gratitude, generosity, patience and self-trust to create greater happiness and a purposeful, passionate life.

For more information about M.J., visit www.mj-ryan.com.

CHAPTER 5

✦

CREATIVE VOIDS AND TIME TRIALS

It's hard enough to try to mentally keep yourself motivated when you're lonely, relying solely on your talent to bring you joy. And dinner. And probably health insurance. But when you can't use that talent for one reason or another, feelings of worthlessness can set in. And for many creatives, the time between gigs—or even having too much to do—can be downright depressing because many question their worth and ability to make business thrive at all.

The concept of balance resonates for so many creatively self-employed people. Without it, surviving down time can be hellish. There's no one to even you out in this business—no cubicle to hide in while you come out of your funk. You can't simply show up for eight hours; you have to *earn* your living. Time is everything to freelancers—having too much, having too little. Months, days, hours, minutes. Heck, we even bill by time. So when you're stuck and can't come up with any ideas, or you have ideas and don't have any work prospects, it can be frustrating.

In this chapter, we'll explore how you can stay afloat during time trials, and even make them easier on yourself. We'll learn by seeing how others do so.

The Many Hats of the Creatively Self-Employed

Penelope Dullaghan, a South Carolina-based illustrator focusing on editorial, advertising and fine art, knows that the creative self-employment balancing act can be just as maddening as being trapped behind a desk in the 9-to-5 world. "Being self-employed requires you to wear lots of hats … artistic, business, office manager, intern, go-getter, account manager and agent," says Dullaghan. "Balancing my time and attending to each role isn't something that comes naturally."

That's why Dullaghan has had to learn that when illustration work is not coming in, for example, it's important to focus on other aspects of business. She uses that time to focus on self-promotion and respond to client feedback.

But learning to go with the ebb and flow of self-employment isn't easy. When that first lapse between projects hits, many creatives panic. If you're not working, after all, you're not earning money. And because you're in charge of your work flow, you may blame yourself for it not coming in.

When she's not on creative down time, Dullaghan is busy as ever for a number of clients including *The Indianapolis Star*, Evite and Resort Condominiums International. But what is a girl (or guy) to do between jobs? There are plenty of other business-related tasks you'll learn about in Chapter 9. The important thing to know right now is that creative voids are normal, inevitable and useful.

On the other side of the time spectrum is the possibility of working too much. Aside from not having enough work, there are times when many creatives are flooded. Swamped. This is another aspect of creative self-employment that many have experienced. When you get a new opportunity for work, you most likely have about 10 other things on your plate. You think that it may be okay to say no, as you're snowed under and would like to take care of yourself. But then you remember times of work famine: wondering when a gig would come in, feeling desperate for money as your safety funds dwindle. So you take the job, adding it to your already overwhelming schedule.

The result? Burnout, baby.

"When you're self-employed, you really own your success (and your failure), so it's very easy to work yourself like a dog and forget to refill that creative cup. I'm still struggling with this," says Dullaghan, who starts most mornings working and doesn't stop until the night. Though she's trying to break the habit, she confesses that fear of failure and the inability to say no have led her to some exhausting weeks.

But she doesn't miss the 9-to-5 world. Not at all. "I never feel guilty for not being in the corporate world, mainly because I'm working harder now than I ever did then," says Dullaghan. "Freelancing is not easy. I feel like it would be a lot easier to coast by at a 9-to-5 job with steady paychecks and retirement plans and lunch hours."

Time for Work

Long hours or work deprivation aside—heck, even when you don't have any inspiration—time is of the essence for creatives. But most wouldn't trade their sometimes unstable creative career for the world. Holly DeWolf, an illustrator from Canada, is one of those people. Although she misses the regular paychecks, she says 9-to-5 life was definitely not for her.

But just because she's not in that world does not mean that time isn't an issue for the mother of two. She says not being able to work enough is a hindrance. With kids and a husband who also works at home, someone has to handle chores. Having a sitter in during the week helps DeWolf to get some quiet time to get things done, but still, there are never enough hours in the day. "I could use an extra five hours to my day to get everything done," says DeWolf. "Some days I have to just deal with the fact that not everything on the list is going to get finished. I have learned to make those lists a little smaller."

Another time factor that affects DeWolf (and, I think all of us) is the need for breaks as we work. I recall that sitting at my desk job was not so bad when I had to be there from 9-to-5 each day. I had the Internet to keep me busy when I wasn't doing work stuff, and I had the Internet to distract me from the mundane tasks when I was. It was a real adjustment for me going into self-employment when I actually wanted to work. After a good hour of intense work, I was exhausted. Why? Because I was putting my all into it. That's when Starbucks breaks became a necessity. And the necessities fluctuate for me—sometimes I need a cup of tea, sometimes I need to work out. Sometimes I need to venture in to the living room and catch up on a soap or take a nap. Sometimes I simply need to pull away from the desk for a few moments.

"When I start to get run down or in need of a break then I start to procrastinate. Taking mini-vacations and stepping away from my desk helps a lot," says DeWolf. "I am a fairly motivated person but there are days where that creative side just doesn't happen. Those are the days that I need to say 'good enough' and walk away for a while."

For DeWolf, those moments of de-stressing go a long way to help her get revitalized. It figures; because creatives are running on their own juice as opposed to performing robotic tasks, the work can really wipe us out!

Debating 9-to-5 Life Again

Sometimes, the thought of a 9-to-5 job can sound like a dream. At least it did for Monica Lee after she got divorced and closed her greeting card company. "I had a small child to support, and I couldn't sit still enough in my sorrow to even imagine illustrating," says Lee, who went back to work as a flight attendant to regroup after her divorce.

But when she attended a Society of Children's Book Writers and Illustrators conference, she got her self-employment bug back. She had always wanted to follow her dream of being an illustrator, but for a while other obligations had to take over. "Fortunately, I have been able to get back to illustration and design slowly," says Lee, who currently lives in Massachusetts and works as an illustrator and designer. Inky Antics, a rubber-stamping company, licensed her drawings in 2005.

Lee still works as a flight attendant sometimes because of its tangible income benefits, but has found great joy and possibility in licensing her funky designs. She's created a portfolio, fashioned a website and begun to market herself. She's even illustrated a few well-known young adult book covers.

So what keeps this mom going? "My favorite thing is the actual work," says Lee. "Sometimes I look at something I have done and say, 'How did I do that?' Like when you get in your car and suddenly you are at your destination with no recall of how you got there. Color, paints, paper, even the computer art make time stop for me!"

Lee has chosen to immerse herself in work. She is an avid creator, even when her work hasn't been commissioned. Sure, down time to market her business and work on licensing deals is important, but for her, going back to the roots works best.

Jennifer Hill, a graphic designer from Massachusetts, hasn't returned to 9-to-5 life. She worked for a major beauty company as a designer for two years after she graduated from college. "I was always late," says Hill, who tries not to work on weekends. "I hated not having control of my own schedule … being at the whim of someone else's schedule."

She said there were many reasons why she left her 9-to-5 job, but is much happier being able to sleep later and make her own schedule. She usually works from about 10 a.m. to 7 p.m. each day, depending on project flow. Hill is proof that our hours can be just as much, if not more, demanding than that of the 9-to-5-ers. Sometimes freelancers can't break the 9-to-5 work hours, and it makes good sense to work the same hours as those in corporate jobs. After all, it's when the rest of the world is at work.

Neil Tortorella works mostly 9-to-5 handling Web design and copywriting for his Ohio-based business, Tortorella Design. But that doesn't mean he's a 9-to-5 kind of guy. On the contrary, as someone from a line of self-employed family members, working for himself seems to come naturally to Tortorella. "I'm something of a creature of habit, so I lean toward working set hours," he says. "I don't consider project work my only work time. Administrative tasks, marketing and such also fall under the 'work' moniker."

That's why he works on marketing tasks for an hour or so before business hours, after getting up early each day. Based on his to-do list, he determines how long he will work on each project scheduled for the day. Sometimes he even plans it out the night before. I was amazed at how much organization and thought goes into his day. It took me years of frustration to set my schedule and realize that I couldn't just "do" assignments; I had to organize them.

Time is so vital to freelancers, because you can be bored one day and inundated the next. Tortorella has learned to steady it all. "How we structure our working hours requires balance," he says. "Not working enough productive hours will certainly put our business in jeopardy. On the flip side, if we're working 80-plus hours per week, we need to ask ourselves why. Odds are, we might need to get a book or take a course on time management."

Hours That Kill

Jackie Alpers, a fine art photographer and photo editor, says she hopes she never has to go back to 9-to-5 work either. (Though, she points out, it's more like 8-to-6 for most people. True, true.)

"Those types of jobs are a detriment to society," says Alpers, who lives in Arizona. "People are so caught up in the working world that they never get to pursue their life." She remembers being so exhausted when she got home from her full-time job that she couldn't do anything but drink wine and vege out in front of the television. There was no time—or energy—for art or writing, her two passions, or to even go out and see a band play. "I really think that the 9-to-5 work environment sucks the life out of people," says Alpers. Most of us agree. That's why we do just about anything to keep freelance work flowing in, and sometimes turn our backs on taking care of ourselves to do so.

Working too hard is a struggle for many creatives. Tim Benzinger, a graphic designer from Connecticut, says time has always been difficult to deal with. "The hardest thing about being self-employed is restricting yourself," says Benzinger. "There have been many times where I find myself working late at night, accepting calls at any hour of the day, or cramming my schedule with too much work. I love what I do and working late doesn't seem to bother me much until it becomes a normal occurrence."

When he is overworked, Benzinger gets irritable, tired and says he can't think straight. This affects the people around him. "No one, including yourself, should have to deal with this. Working is important, but not to the point where it hurts me and others," he says.

Benzinger has overcome this by limiting what he does. For example, he tries not to accept work calls after 6:30 p.m. at night. And if he gets an e-mail for a project, he doesn't respond until the next day. Although he tries not to work more than 40 hours a week, he says there have been times when he works 75 hours a week. When he is overworked, he says the creative ideas that he needs to provide for his clients don't come as easy. And it limits him from accepting new projects that could further propel his career.

"The best thing to do is plan each week ahead of time and stick to that schedule," he says. "The thing about being self-employed is that you are the boss. The hardest boss to overcome is yourself. Once you do, life becomes stress free, you have more time to spend with friends and family and, believe it or not, you are taken more seriously." Benzinger calls it restricting; I refer to what he does as self-discipline. Because when I've set boundaries for myself, which felt artificial at first, I found that I took care of myself more. I couldn't tell when I was slipping into an overworked state of frenzy until it was too late. So it *is* important to set limits.

"Most of my clients don't get upset when I tell them I don't work weekends, or I let something rest until the next workday. There is a sense of respect that you gain from your clients. You are all the sudden more professional to them instead of just a person free every hour of the day." Good to know, because once business starts taking off, like you'll see with our next creative, setting boundaries is vital.

When Freelance *Is* Steady

Alma de la Rosa, a rubber stamp designer who owns her own company, The Cat's Pajamas, actually left the corporate world for more steady work, and has found it in her own business. Previously an advertising art director, she worked on a few accounts at a time. But when those clients left the company, as many do after three to five years, she wound up leaving, too. She was laid off at the time she decided to go into business for herself.

"What made me leave the corporate world for good was that I just got tired of looking for jobs and wanted something more stable. I also got tired of creating things that I hated. I felt that I had become a hack and I wanted to create things that I liked," explains de la Rosa, who lives in California. Now she does that, but says she doesn't log hours because she doesn't want to know how many hours she works per week. Though she tells her customers she works 10 a.m. to 5 p.m., her day varies. Sometimes she leaves during those hours to run errands, but always keeps the fax and answering machines on to take orders. This gives her time to get away from her workspace.

"I generally work several hours before having a late dinner and possibly one to two hours after," says de la Rosa. "I almost always work on weekends." Would you call her a workaholic? It's okay—she acknowledges being one. "I definitely have always considered myself a workaholic. I am happiest working. I feel like I am accomplishing something. But, I also know that I am a great procrastinator, too. And, I am a workaholic in that way, too. I work at procrastinating."

The Procrastination Blues

Anita Firebaugh, a writer from Virginia, understands procrastination and practices regularly. Most creatives work too hard, don't get enough work in or gaze away when work rests in front of them. And there's nothing wrong with procrastination—some of us actually work better under pressure. It's just another difference between people.

"The hardest thing about being self-employed for me is not having someone look over my shoulder," says Firebaugh. "While I seem to need someone looking over my shoulder sometimes, at the same time I despise being bossed around."

There is no easy balance, is there?

"Being my own taskmaster is difficult," she continues. "When I worked for other people, I was very cognizant of the fact that I was being paid to do something with my time. At my office (a converted bedroom in my home) I expect myself to be doing something—and that seems to translate to most anything from looking out the window to answering e-mail."

When she has a project with a deadline, things are pretty smooth. She can put aside other work and get down to business. But when she has time on her hands, the possibilities are endless. "The laundry, some days, looks more inviting than the keyboard," says Firebaugh.

She exhibits a raw honesty that I found refreshing. She says that she didn't enjoy the 9-to-5 world, but also confesses to needing some sort of supervisor to keep herself in check. "I am not a good boss to myself," she says. "Sometimes I work myself very hard and if it were someone else doing that to me, I would quit!" I think she'll eventually become her own best supervisor.

Violette Clark acknowledges that she is a bit of a procrastinator, too. The Canada-based painter, illustrator and art educator has so many creative endeavors cooking at any given time that it's sometimes hard to stay on track. What is hardest about being creatively self-employed for Clark isn't the loss of steady paychecks or water-cooler talks, but the distractions that exist.

"I'm a big procrastinator," says Clark, whose home, dubbed the "magic cottage" has garnered attention worldwide because of its splashy colors and lively images. (Head over to her website—you should see her one-of-a-kind car, too!)

Whether it's a cup of tea, a telephone call, an e-mail or browsing websites, Clark says that the menagerie of creative ideas and physical distractions can take away from her work. That's why having deadlines is best for her. But she knows she doesn't have to go to a 9-to-5 job to have the self-discipline necessary to get work done. "Having a boss would be a good motivator; however … it would make me more frustrated—sort of like a catch-22. I need to be accountable, but somehow need a coach encouraging me and guiding me on."

Even though distractions get in the way, I like to think of it as part of her creative process. It makes her authentic. And it's how *she* works best.

Re-Energizing During Down Time

For Tine Wiggens, freelancing has been a rewarding—but very personal—struggle. She was working as a sales clerk in a home décor retail store and not happy with the mundane tasks of the job. When she imagined giving advice to a friend in her situation, she says that she would have told the buddy not to waste his or her time and talents there. So she started thinking about taking her own guidance.

"I talked things through with my husband, and a few days later I gave my notice and was outta there," says Wiggens, a jewelry and mixed-media designer from Canada. "It was the best advice I have ever given [myself], and I do not look back or regret it, not for a single second. Now I am trying as hard as I can, with my motivator being not having to go back into retail."

But freelancing has its ups and downs, and Wiggens is not one to deny it. The unsteady paychecks are a hardship for her, as is the struggle to create her line of Soul Bird jewelry and mixed-media pieces. She says that she doubts herself when work doesn't come in steadily, or when she simply feels uninspired.

"I think it's like a natural reflex unless, of course, for some for whom money is not an issue," says Wiggens. When her creativity ebbs, Wiggens says, she makes use of the time by trying to re-energize herself. She goes over ideas she collects in her sketchbook, trying new media to create art. She makes time for researching new avenues for her art and updates her website. "I explore new things, ideas and designs. I trust that it is like with the tide coming in and going out knowing that the next high tide will come. And it usually does."

What helps Wiggens boost her creative juices is her Web-based project Studio Friday. At the end of each week, she posts a creative prompt and, through her blog, has gotten other artists involved in sharing their creations. Participants post their work each Friday, as does she, which makes for good socializing online and, of course, more inspiration.

I like Wiggens' outlook because she sees that there is a natural up and down to creative work. But she uses the time to her advantage and *trusts* that she'll still come out on top. Easy to do? Nope. (I'm still learning to do that, too.) But I guess after you get through so many storms and come out alive, you realize that it won't kill you to take a day off when you have nothing to do, or that you need to spend time taking care of administrative tasks for your business to prosper. Just because you're not actively working on your trade doesn't mean you're not working. Think of marketing tactics, read up on the industry or get updated on your filing or your finances; these are all great ways to use down time.

*   *   *

Benzinger used to worry about not getting enough work. He does use down time to revive himself and explore new creative endeavors. "When work doesn't come in steady, I read a lot, I try new things and open my eyes to what's out there. I could be learning anything from a new style of design, to how to cook one mean spaghetti meal. Without my drive to learn new things, I wouldn't have learned the process of screen printing, I wouldn't have started a clothing label, started a design studio, or a paper goods business. When I have down time, it seems to always pay off in the end," he says.

Of course when he was starting out and getting used to running a business, he wasn't as sure that there was an advantage to down time. "Being self-employed, you have to be confident in what you do. You know what you are capable of, and if you are passionate about what you do, you are capable of anything," Benzinger says. "Taking risks is also something you can't be afraid of. So many opportunities have passed me by in the past because I wouldn't take risks. There were many times where I had dry work months, or times where I was overloaded with work. It's all part of being self-employed, and learning what works for you is half the battle."

The Need to Relax

Using her down time to personally recharge has worked well for Claudine Hellmuth, a mixed-media artist from Florida. When she's not busy licensing her artwork to various companies, she teaches workshops about mixed-media collage techniques. She also has written two books. It sounds like she shouldn't have *any* down time with so many things going for her, but like the other creatives you've read about in this chapter, lapses in time without work are normal, if not imminent, for Hellmuth.

"If I am having a slow time I start to worry, 'Will my business keep going, how will I make money in the future, etc.,'" she says. "Work is just about all I think of all the time. I have a hard time feeling good about time that I spend that is not work related."

When she can chill out a little bit, she reads, visits friends and watches movies. "With my work, it seems to be feast or famine—it's either flooding in or there's nothing. So in the down times I try to recharge and then calm myself down by reminding myself that the work will come again, like it always does." Her words ring true. You can only stop flipping out about not having work to do after you've gone through the low point and come back up successfully. Like shampooing, it's a rinse-and-repeat process. Eventually, hopefully, we start to take it easy on ourselves when life isn't so hectic. (Sound familiar? This is the "creative process" we talked about in Chapter 4.)

In some cases, we can even learn to enjoy our down time, whether we use it to market ourselves or personally rejuvenate. It took me a few ebb-and-flow periods to realize that it was okay to take a break. If I had nothing to do, or if I had too much on my plate, I could control my schedule and make the most of my time—I just had to stay on top of it.

Kristen King, a freelance writer-editor from Virginia, has a hard time giving herself breaks as well. (Clearly she's not the only Kristen with this issue!) For her, taking sick time and vacation days can be difficult. You would think it would be easy for many creatives to take an afternoon off or take a mid-week vacation—but not always. Why? Because we can be our own worse enemies, especially when we're worried about making ends meet and realizing we have to be the ones to get things done to make that happen.

"I'm a really tough boss," says King. "I have extremely high expectations for myself, and I have a tendency toward perfectionism." Although those are great qualities for running her own business, she also struggles with it in the form of balancing her professional expectations with her personal limitations.

*   *   *

Hill, mentioned previously in this chapter, says that every August puts her in a funk. "Summertime is a slow time, and usually around August I start having a mini-breakdown about money," explains the designer, who specializes in retail, restaurants and other creative ventures. It's usually around that time that her boyfriend reminds her she has this issue every August, and things always turn around for her in September.

Knowing your patterns is a great asset. For Hill, she planned a lot of travel this past summer because she knew things would slow down. That didn't help her finances, but with a job that affects her so personally, I think it was a smart idea. Hill's insight is interesting because it's an example of how knowing yourself and your schedule are vital to staying sane—and successful. After trial and error, she knows her patterns, and came up with a simple way to avoid a mental low that would have otherwise held her down.

I do this, too. After about two days of not having anything fresh I begin to panic. It wasn't until this happened several times that I learned this was *part* of the creative process. Sometimes I still freak out. Like Hill, I have a very special man in my life who reminds me that things will pick up. It's happened so many times that Tim usually just gives a chuckle now, and I know my worries are pointless.

Half the battle, at least for me, to overcoming the trials of creative self-employment involved watching myself go through cycles. When I would be alarmed over not having any new work come in and a few days later watch as I got overloaded again, I learned that the lull never lasted long. So what was the point in worrying? I was doing everything I could to bring in business. And after a while, I trusted that it would come in. I trusted the process.

I think part of the process is going through these cycles. When you see that you emerge better than ever every time, you get fed up with the worry. You eventually let go of it and move on to healthier thoughts.

Parental Timing

Many creative types I spoke to not only had to worry about setting a schedule and making it through creative dry spots, but they had to take care of kids, too. While it is nice to be at home with children, this creates an issue for many freelancers.

Cynthia Potts, a freelance writer from New York, loves writing for newspapers and magazines, but admits that taking care of her family dictates how much time she can devote to her craft. "The hardest thing about being self-employed is time management," says Potts. "I have two small children, so balancing caring for them and working can be tricky. Some days the work has to wait, and other times the kids have to entertain themselves. It's a constant struggle." She works every day but Sunday and can work around her children's naps and play times. At times, though, she spends all night in front of the computer.

Jennifer Hollowell, an artist and writer mentioned in Chapter 4, also struggles to provide care for her children and while maintaining her career. Her work hours were more regular when her children were in daycare. Now that they're in school, she will have a good block of hours for peaceful work. "Time management will get easier and more routine without schedules overlapping," says Hollowell.

Sticking to a Schedule

Regardless what type of routine freelancers have, it's best to keep some sort of schedule, says Ben Dattner, founder of Dattner Consulting. He deals with many types of workers through his New York–based organizational consulting and research firm, which helps groups and individuals to evaluate and enhance psychological, social and political dynamics.

"Set times in the day when, for example, you step away from your computer to read, write, paint or engage in other activities that require greater focus than is possible when multitasking," Dattner suggests.

Routine may sound mundane, especially if you're new to the world of creative self-employment. Of course it does—half of the fun of freelancing is being able to pick up and leave when you want to. Although that is a definite luxury of the job, it can be difficult to get things done when you're trotting around running errands and even taking breaks. For me, I found that e-mail and housework became distractions. It was fun to check e-mail during the day as much as I could. And the housework had to get done. But then I got into bouts where I would multitask so much in a day that it was hard to focus. I would get frustrated and my productivity expired.

Setting a schedule helped me a lot. Because you're your own boss, you don't have to 9-to-5 it. You can work mornings if that's best for you, or evenings if you're a night owl. Me? I usually thrive on a mid-day break and then finish out the afternoon strong. I leave the nights to work with looming deadlines and relaxing. It all depends on what I have on my plate, but having a clear plan of what I at least *want* my day to look like helps me work efficiently so I can take those breaks completely guilt free.

The key to overcoming our time management issues is to plan how we use our time. You can still pick up and go out for that spontaneous jog or cup or coffee (that will always be a perk of creative self-employment!). But set a schedule for yourself and treat your creative endeavor as a company. Make it a *fun* business, but don't forget to make time to schedule breaks. This will help you overcome the creative voids and time trials that every creative faces.

CREATIVE PROFILE
Penelope Dullaghan
Illustrator
Columbia, South Carolina

Getting Started
Penelope Dullaghan was an art director for an advertising agency, where she hired illustrators. She started taking on projects herself, and began craving full-time illustrative work. She freelanced for a year to build up her portfolio and client base before going the freelance route.

Taking "the Leap"
As far as becoming creatively self-employed, Penelope says: "It came down to 'now or never,' and I did it." She now focuses her business on editorial, advertising and fine art.

Inexpensive Adventures
Penelope re-evaluated her spending habits since becoming self-employed. She says she's learned to do inexpensive things for fun, like having a picnic with her husband instead of going out to eat, or going to the library instead of buying a book. She even created a section on her website in hopes of sharing ideas with others and adding more ideas to her database of inexpensive escapades.

For more information about Penelope, visit
www.penelopeillustration.com.

CHAPTER 6

✦

ISOLATIONISM

Every creatively self-employed worker knows that the feeling of being independent can be extremely liberating. You come and go as you please. You can work when you want. You can paint your toenails while on the phone with a client. Heck, some creatives even handle phone interviews in the buff. But when the rush wears off, many self-employed folks find themselves craving human contact.

There are no cubicles in a home office, no water-cooler discussions, no company outings, and no office gossip to be amused by. That's why feeling isolated can mentally wear on many creatives who are naturally social creatures. Sure, some of us are isolationists who prefer to stay in the dark and paint or write without coming up for food or a tooth-brushing, but it's nice to have the *option* of socializing while you work. And working as many of us do—at home, or in an office alone—means that the outlets once available are no longer there. Like so many aspects of creative self-employment discussed in this book, combating the trials is only a matter of getting support, or at least, in this case, a lunch pal or coffee buddy to break up the day.

When I began working from home, I was on a high. But I found that soon I also felt extremely lonely. Inside, I was craving the fun antics I used to have at work, even in the office where I was not content with my job. My coworkers were wonderful, quirky and helped make the long hours fly by. But I was fed up with the lack of money and unreasonable hours—and an abundance of inept bosses—so I had to leave even though I knew I'd miss my colleagues.

But then, pleased with what I was doing as a freelance writer, it was hard to admit that there were parts of my dream job that I didn't like … such as accounting and sales. What was worse than the isolationism was trying to cope with these muddled feelings of discouragement. How could something horrible come with something so wonderful as my dream job becoming a reality? Could the bad exist with the good?

Someone once told me that no job is perfect. Still, once I got my ideal job, I could not believe that it wasn't as ideal as I had imagined. I knew that seclusion was an aspect of the job I didn't enjoy, and after weeks of feeling lonely and thinking I was doomed to a life of solitude, I came to my senses and realized that there was hope.

I could create my own social life. In fact, I could create my own support system to combat the shortcoming of the job, I thought to myself. Like most of the troublesome aspects of my job as a copywriter, I had to take proactive measures to remedy these issues. In the end, realizing that you have to create your own social life is essential. It's a fundamental component to help you work at your best.

Human contact, especially with those who understand the trials of creative self-employment, may not come with the job. But taking the initiative to be more social will surely help you work—and feel—better.

Feeling the "Lonelies"

When Andrea Scher began her jewelry business, things were sort of rocky. She was college educated, and had the opportunity to work with author Susan Ariel Rainbow Kennedy (SARK) for five years. So when she found the courage to go into business selling her creations and it was just her, it was difficult to adjust.

"For me, the hardest thing about being self-employed is the 'lonelies,'" says the California jewelry maker and owner of Superhero Designs. "It was most acute at the beginning, when I had everything and nothing to do each day. Very few clients took up my time, no appointments, the only energy generated in the business had to come from me. And this was scary!"

She learned during her first year of business that beneath the loneliness were fears that her endeavor wasn't going to work, or that she'd go broke. She even feared her work was not good enough. Luckily, things turned around for Scher. She found that creating her chunky, colorful necklaces brought her great joy. When the orders were flowing in and clients were popping by her website to shop, she wasn't lonely anymore.

"Maybe in the end it was just plain fear masquerading as loneliness that made things so hard for so long," wonders Scher. Whatever it was that made the beginning tough on her, she managed to pull through it with support. In the end, it was the love of her craft, and putting it out into the world, that helped her gain confidence. "I love making the jewelry, holding it in my hand and infusing each piece with my spirit," she says. "I take that part of my craft really seriously. I love the satisfaction of knowing who the piece is for and having that personal connection."

Scher attributes much of her sociability to her website, where she not only sold jewelry, but also posted a blog. It featured photos, personal essays, quotes and anything else that inspired her. "I felt like the blog was a deeper, fuller, wider expression of who I am," Scher says. Soon after, e-mails began to pour in from others who were inspired by her ability to put not only her feelings, but also her photography, out there.

"There was something bigger I was trying to express, something bigger I wanted to contribute," Scher recalls. "I realized that people were inspired by the simple fact that I was doing it, making a living from my art, doing something I loved, and creating it from nothing."

Connecting with others helped her during her trying time. Scher says she was always most satisfied during tough spots when she was mentoring others along the way, getting messages from others who said that she had given them the faith they needed to pursue their own artistic aspirations.

As she continues to make scrumptious jewelry, she has more recently taken on another creative endeavor: life coaching. I would have featured her under that profession, but Scher speaks so prolifically and helpfully about the trials of working alone that she is much more of an asset telling of her raw, explicit truths gleaned directly from her own artistic attempts.

Leaving the Pond

Holly Becker, an interior design consultant from New Hampshire, says that loneliness is the only drawback to self-employment. Even so, she does not regret leaving her 9-to-5 job after nearly 10 years there.

"I find it hard to simply be alone all day. In many ways, I love having space to explore my creativity without interruption. I enjoy being able to wear yoga pants and a t-shirt all day. It's fun to shower at 10 a.m. if I want to," says Becker. "However, the hardest part is giving up the social connections that I had at work: dishing with my colleagues, creative think-tanking in board rooms, staying out until midnight over martinis discussing a project. When I left the pond, I left behind the fish."

Becker is trying to strike a balance by attending professional functions such as trade shows and gallery events. She even meets with designers she interviews. She also has used www.mediabis-tro.com's writing workshop to network and found it very helpful. "It was so energizing and resulted in a developing friendship with a very tuned-in writer that has a slew of connections," she says. "And unlike many writers out there, she actually doesn't mind helping those of us that are new to the world of freelance."

Just as many creatives use support to help build their confidence and rejection resilience, it's important to reach out for support when you are in the position of working by yourself creatively.

When Denise Biondo left her 9-to-5 job, she also found herself missing the social aspect of the gig. The job wasn't too creative, so leaving the administrative tasks behind wasn't too hard. Besides, she would play around with graphics on the computer anyway, which added a little enjoyment to her day. But leaving work buddies behind was difficult.

"In the beginning, I had quite a bit of anxiety about [self-employment] because I had no idea what I was doing and never seriously considered working for myself. I was so used to the 9-to-5 world that I thought I was just taking an extended vacation from reality," says Biondo, a graphic designer based in New York.

But the lonelies crept in for her, too. She confesses that the hardest thing about creative self-employment for her is being alone and working at home. "Usually, going to a place of work every day puts you in a different mind frame. It is a team environment and you share the experience with other people and there are different people who handle different aspects of the business," she explains. "[Now] you look at the clock and you're still in your pajamas at lunch time." Her husband was a huge support, and though she still misses the social aspect of working, Biondo has become immersed in the challenges and possibilities that her business brings.

The Need to Connect

Having a support system to relate to and help you build confidence is not only helpful, but necessary. It provides you with good business ideas and support, *and* it gets creatives socializing together.

"Interaction with others is important," notes Evelyn Windley Kaufman, a life coach from Kentucky. "We are wired for relationships and connections." She says that contact is important for creatives, and she knows so personally. When she worked in a corporate setting, Windley Kaufman could stop by someone's office or bump into a friend in the hall. But since she started her life coaching business and began working for herself, mostly from home, she has to be more strategic about connecting with others. She uses e-mail to stay in touch, and also makes what she refers to as "spot calls," two- to three-minute calls to get in touch with friends and colleagues. Workwise, she confers monthly with other coaches by telephone. She also makes time to meet friends for coffee or lunch when she can.

"A support system is vital," says Windley Kaufman. "With the technology that's available, it's easy to connect and receive support." Very true. But what if the rest of your friends are slaving away at their 9-to-5's while you're ready to socialize at noon? Even if you can't meet a friend in person, the Internet offers forums, chat rooms and blogs to stay connected to others. And when you interact with a community or cyber avenue that puts you in touch with other creatives, you'll make friends in no time.

Why? Not only are those creatives probably lonely, too, but they will most likely understand all the quirks of your job that your 9-to-5 friends just don't get.

CREATIVE PROFILE
Andrea Scher
Jewelry Maker and Life Coach
Berkeley, California

Getting Started

Andrea Scher worked for author Susan Ariel Rainbow Kennedy (SARK) before starting her jewelry-making business, Superhero Designs. She creates chunky, colorful beaded jewelry, and is a certified life coach.

Business Logistics

There are advantages to having an online business as opposed to selling wholesale to retailers, says Andrea. A lot of artists will only sell their work to retail boutiques and department stores around the country. This means that to make money, they need to sell in bulk. To keep up with demand, they need to hire people to assemble the jewelry, either here or abroad. "This is one way of doing business, but not the route I chose to take," she says.

Another Passion

"Part of my enthusiasm for life coaching stems from my own experience working with a coach. I have always wanted to write a book, but had never been able to complete a book proposal. My coach not only created a system of accountability for me, but coached me through the places that had stopped me over and over again," recalls Andrea.

"In six weeks I had completed the proposal and submitted it to a publishing company. Whether the book gets published or not, this was an incredible victory for me."

For more information about Andrea, visit www.superherodesigns.com.

CHAPTER 7

✦

GOING CRAZY

With all of the black and white issues that creatives face, there are bound to be some gray areas as well. By gray, I mean that aside from the business issues, creative self-employment can wear on us emotionally. Because our work is so personal, it's not like having a bad day at work when your proposal is turned down. In the creatively self-employed world, your work is your livelihood. And when it doesn't seem to be going well, it can feel like it is spiraling downward—and taking you with it.

Rejection can turn into poor self-esteem.

Loneliness can translate into depression.

Dry spells can create anxiousness.

For some people, experiencing such a wide range of personal trials can leave them with some emotional issues, especially if there are other vulnerabilities under the surface. Even if a creative does not have to head to a shrink for solace, that doesn't mean that the stresses they face can't drive them a little nutty. Personally, I've faced many days as a manic mess and sought professional coaching to help me deal with the stressors of the job. In this chapter, we'll explore some of the emotional struggles that creatives face and offer hope to help you tame any inner—and outer—critics.

Lie down on the couch and feel the next few pages of free therapy take you away … and bring you back to an even better place.

The Terror of Self-Employment

After Michelle Ponto, a freelance writer from Canada, quit her job and immersed herself in freelance life, she freaked out a little. "The first six months were scary," confesses Ponto. "I woke up with cold sweats, panic attacks, and lived in constant fear of wondering if I could pull it off."

This isn't uncommon. After all, leaving stable ground—as much as you prepare for it—can be downright frightening. For Ponto, she didn't doubt her talent, but was concerned about making money using it. She quit her job cold turkey, which probably added to the angst. "The hardest thing is not knowing when the next paycheck is going to arrive," she says. "Unlike a full-time job, [when you're self-employed] money doesn't magically appear in your bank account every two weeks. You have to seek it out yourself. I'm still struggling to overcome this, but the only solution I have is to keep working. Somehow the money always turns up and the bills get paid."

Regardless of how we leave our stable 9-to-5 jobs and move into self-employment, there are bound to be emotionally difficult times. Because self-employment means that no one is feeding you paychecks and health insurance, it can be scary to think of not having them. Because of this, creatives put more pressure on themselves to succeed—we kind of have to.

But what most people aren't talking about are times like the ones Ponto experienced (and was so brave enough to tell us about!). I hope her story can help another creative feel less alone when it comes down to those sleepless nights and mid-day snaps. What's her advice? The same solution to just about every conundrum mentioned so far in this book. Let time pass. "After a while, you adjust to living on the edge and it's great," says Ponto, who is now getting international clients and enjoying her freedom.

I'd like to add that creatives will not also necessarily have unstable jobs. The beginning can be a little rocky. Once business builds, you won't have to market your services as much, and a steady flow of work will come in.

*   *   *

Holly Becker, who shared with us in the previous chapter, experiences anxiety when she feels a creative block. She says that as soon as she stretches, drinks some orange juice and puts on some good music, she finds she can get back on track and unclog her creative block. "When you feel anxious, you have to tap into why you are feeling that way," she offers. "Think about what is causing the feeling. Try to control your feelings."

Although Becker says that she is not a very emotional person, she confesses that her emotional training took years. "I use to cry in the restroom at work when someone didn't agree with something I said during a meeting," she says. "Growing a second skin, one that cannot be easily penetrated, is a must."

As a professional blogger, she also deals with the general public. And sometimes, a nasty comment can be devastating. For a while, she says, she was confounded by mean comments left by readers. But in time, it reminded her that people were threatened by her success, and the negativity blew over.

Many creatives have blogs, so putting one's heart out for all to read can mean dealing with rejection there—or downright rude people who can be jealous. Luckily for Becker, the anxiety passed and she continues to experience success with her online journal.

Do It All—Everything!

Most people I interviewed for this book said the fear of not making enough money was what caused them the most angst in this business. Rightfully so. But for others, just the nature of the job is enough to drive anyone mad. Why? Because you're not just in one position—you are also handling all the business administrative tasks. And when you put all the must-dos in with trying to keep positive, you can feel a little down from time to time.

Ted Forbes, a freelance designer from California, said his job varies day to day, and because he is a one-man operation, he has had to learn every aspect of running a business, aside from creating brochures, posters and websites. For him, *that's* the easy part—when it comes to filing, accounting and sales, well, he would rather take a nap.

"The hardest thing for me is the fact you have to juggle many job titles. You're the designer, the production person, the courier, the accountant, the manager, the computer repairman and the janitor all in any given day," he says. "Most of these jobs are easy to juggle, but the hardest two are being the creative person and being the businessman." That's because when work is coming in, he feels more comfortable and is more creative.

The back-and-forth routine can turn an otherwise fun job into a frazzled workday. When we are jumping from our accounting tasks to coming up with a clever tagline for an ad campaign get most of us crazed. Creatives can easily lose focus this way as well.

"Then when you get the jobs off your plate, everything comes to a halt because you didn't do any networking, promos, cold calls, etc.," he says. "That's the hardest part—is doing both at once." This is why many creatives are constantly marketing themselves, or at least doing so during down time. With effort, you're likely to have another gig lined up when another ends.

While Forbes hasn't gone off the deep end, I liked his depiction of what life is really like. I saw a lot of my own struggles in what he had to say. I get drained when I am doing too many things at once, and I also freak out when work doesn't come in. In addition, I get so wrapped up in projects that I forget to constantly market myself in between.

Forbes notes that the overall craze of life as a creative freelancer has driven him a little batty. The struggle of it all can sometimes take its toll. "When work is slow it's, 'How will I pay this bill, how will I afford equipment I need, how will I eat, how will I repair my car.' I can't sleep. I get anxious during the day. I feel like a failure. It's tough," he says. "You have to have a support system … one or two people you can talk to who understand what you're going through."

Forbes exudes honesty about feelings that I think most of us go through but never share. After all, when you tell friends you're making it as a writer or artist, you don't mention the days when you feel bummed out, do you? Probably not. Most people may not experience the mood swings that we do.

This is the essence of what I hope you're picking up throughout this book—that it's okay to have these ups and downs and the feelings that go with them. *We've all been there in one way or another.*

I'm not sure if it's being a woman filled with estrogen, or just my personality, but this chapter, this very topic, hits home for me because I'm very prone to anxiety. With some coaching, I've learned how to cope with stress (even the good, overwhelming kind—like when you're publishing a book!). It's my hope that, regardless of whether work starts having a negative impact on your mental health, you'll see that it's perfectly okay to feel a gamut of uplifting, hopeless and thrilling emotions all at the same time. Let's hear some more stories that will illustrate my point.

Using Your Quirks As Assets

Kristen King, also mentioned in Chapter 4, doesn't consider her job stressful enough to cause any mental or physical problems. Actually, setting her own hours and controlling her client workflow puts her in control and eases stress. But she does have attention deficit disorder.

"When I first learned this about myself, I thought it was going to be a major problem," says King, who recently made the push into freelance life after working a full-time 9-to-5 job and juggling about 30 hours a week of freelance work on the side. The 9-to-5 is gone, but she's still in school two nights a week—ironically, in the building directly across the street from her old office—working on her master's degree in publishing.

"Procrastination comes easily to me. It's not that I do not want to sit down and do the work—I just get distracted easily, and it happens equally whether I'm completely alone or surrounded by a busy office environment," says King. For her, ADD has turned into an asset now that she is freelancing full-time.

"I generally have several projects going on at once, so when my mind starts to wander, I switch to working on something else for a while. If proofreading gets slow, I move on to writing a query letter. When I lose steam on an article I'm drafting, I pick up where I left off with substantive editing for a novel manuscript," says King. "Can't stand one more minute of writing or editing? No problem! I get on the phone and start tracking down some sources."

When King realized that her mind naturally changes gears from one thought process to another with little to no lost time, she says she became a phenomenal multitasker. "And it helps that I have a good memory, so I very seldom lose my place in a project even when I have several on my plate," she says. Although she sometimes gets distracted by pursuits not related to work, she just uses a little self-discipline to stay on track. That doesn't mean that some days don't get downright frustrating, but King's keeping it cool. "By and large, I love the work I'm doing, and that makes it easier to stay on task, even if 'staying on task' actually encompasses several tasks," she says.

I fell in love with Kristen's story while putting this book together—and not just because she has a phenomenal first name. I loved the fact that she worked her way up through the writing world, freelanced on the side and finally was able to break free once she was certain that it was the practical time to do so. She was sensible about freelancing, not rushing out of her job only to fall on her face. She thought it through and has even managed to use what could be a discouraging disorder and make it turn into her favor. And she was brave enough to admit her struggle. Sometimes, all you need to do is tell your story and it can free you.

Proactively Banishing Anxiety

As most of the interviewees in this book said, money is an anxiety producer. That's why I admire what Liz Kalloch, an illustrator and graphic designer from California, said about dealing with anxiety. "There have definitely been lean months," she says. She also experiences nervousness when she does not get as many work calls as she'd like.

Her solution may sound obvious, but it's a reminder to follow logic when it comes to overcoming the trials. "What I have discovered works for me is to keep track of where I am financially, keep some money saved for those slow months and be realistic about what I am spending, and then I am not surprised by low finances during a slow period," Kalloch says. She keeps a couple of months worth of expenses in a savings account, which she says "keeps the worry monster at bay."

She also makes sure she stays occupied when things are slow. She often doesn't have time for marketing efforts when she is busy on a project, so time "off" is ideal to keep business flowing.

Coping with "Imposter Syndrome"

Every time I read through an interview while compiling this book, I found a new challenge that I realized I had experienced. So when Amy Mantione, a graphic designer from New York, introduced her concept of "Imposter Syndrome," I knew it was worth discussing.

Have you ever felt like when work was slow to come in, clients and potential clients weren't calling because they'd found you out? As if they discovered you were a horrible artist, writer, photographer or designer, and *that* was why they weren't contacting you for work? Or that you weren't really what you are? That's what she calls "Imposter Syndrome," and boy do I understand what she's talking about! For me, it comes when things have been on the slower side, or even when a client didn't call back right away. My mind would be flooded with worries, and I would compare myself to other "real" copywriters.

"Even when I am swamped with work there is always a black cloud reminding me that it won't last and I will be slow again," Mantione says. "Sometimes I have to convince myself that I am wrong by looking at my samples or my client list for reassurance that I must have done something right."

Her coping mechanism worked for me. I looked at all of my accomplishments and materials I had written. Had a *fake* copywriter written those? Absolutely not. *I couldn't be an imposter*, I thought to myself. Otherwise, I wouldn't have been able to write marketing copy that my clients raved about. So what was that little critical voice that had no other defense? It was the scared voice, and I needed to disprove it, tone it down and turn it off. Luckily, looking back to past successes worked for Mantione, and it worked for me, too. Try it next time you're worried that you might be a phony!

Work-at-Home Feng Shui and Other Ways to Stay Sane

The trials that freelancers face financially would drive anyone over the edge. When you add a crazy schedule to the mix, things are bound to get a little hectic. Joy Deangdeelert, a home accessories and graphic designer from Pennsylvania, tries to limit herself to an eight-hour day, or even a more relaxed seven-hour day. Even when she's in a time crunch, she tries to avoid working weekends. She takes care of herself and tries to avoid stress, and admits to watching other freelance friends work long hours and seeing their personal lives suffer.

What also keeps her balanced is sorting her career from her home life. "I have to be extra conscious to separate work from home since my work does exist within my home," says Deangdeelert. "I stay in my office area all day and never sit on the couch or watch TV during the day. That area is supposed to be 'home' for me and I limit it to nights and weekends."

She says she has gotten anxious and even depressed during slow periods when work isn't coming in too regularly, and that leads us back to the financial realm of freelancer woes. "With freelancing, your paychecks are always of different amounts and come at varying intervals. The stress not only comes from slow periods and less money at times, but it makes me feel like I haven't budgeted myself properly and I'm being irresponsible," says Deangdeelert. "I'm working on learning to set aside money when I'm making a lot of it so I have some extra funds when things are slower."

Although she's faced trials that have given her emotional struggles, Deangdeelert seems to be able to help herself and also discipline herself well. A creative who loves working in her jammies, she sometimes faces uncomfortable feelings that can cause her to doubt herself. "I feel guilty when work is slow and I'm really struggling to get by," she says. "I feel like other people think I should just get a full-time job for the stability and that I'm being unrealistic to work this way."

For many people, worrying about what others think of them can be harmful. If you're fretting about what other people think about your career choice, you've got to find a way to press on. Stick to your guns. Know that it can be hard when others do not understand what you're doing. (People still think I work an hour a day writing books—and that's *it*.) You just have to find supportive people in a similar career to support your dream, because creatives are certainly outnumbered by 9-to-5-ers.

In Deangdeelert's case, even though she experiences these feelings and the subsequent emotions that can drive some creatives to toss in the towel, she is a shining example of someone who can discipline herself to avoid procrastination and burnout.

When it comes to the topic of Feng Shui, Forbes used it to overcome his discipline problem early on in his career. He worked at home, which didn't have a space for his office. "I felt unemployed and guilty every day in the morning when everyone I knew was at work," he says. So he got on the ball and invented a daily ritual that helped him get moving and feel like he was part of the working world. (*He* knows he is—but as for many of us, his friends don't think he does much of anything besides sit home.) Whether you need to get out to *feel* business-like, or you just want to get out, I like his idea.

"Every morning at 8:30 a.m., I had to be at Starbucks," he says. "I'd just get coffee, sit in the window and sketch out my plan for the day. It worked like a charm. Rush hour crowd is always coming in, so you feel part of the action. You're productive because you're planning your schedule. Then you go back to the 'office' ready to work rather than sleeping in."

Forbes said it was the best career move he ever made. I agree, not only because he got a delectable coffee each day, but also because he did a simple thing that turned his whole day, and his mood, around. I do the same, as I'm sure many of you do. Sometimes you just have to break up the day a little … change the scenery. If you're blocked and starting to feel like an agoraphobic, do try it.

"Later the coffee was getting expensive, but I was well into a groove by the time I stopped [going]," says Forbes. I like his idea of getting out of the house. And you know I *love* that he chose Starbucks as the place to go. I love even more that he is the shining example of one of the "Starbucks people" (see Chapter 1) I was always intrigued by before I became creatively self-employed.

If, like Forbes, you want to spend your hard-earned cash on something a little more permanent than a $4 latte, do what I did: Buy a small espresso machine. Set it up in your work area or office as a way to reward yourself for getting to work (and to entice you to go there on days that you're just not feeling it), or put it somewhere else in your home so you can get out of bed, go for coffee and then take it straight to work with you.

The Drive to Stay Positive

Let's face it: This business is tough, and in difficult times, it's not so hard to feel gloomy. For many of us, it's automatically where our minds go. I'm one of these people. I have a predisposition to pessimism when it comes to believing in myself. It's only through time, and trying to retrain my brain to think positively, that I've been able to blossom in this business.

As I mentioned in the beginning of this book, I faced what I thought were insurmountable periods of doubt and frustration when I began. I didn't realize that feeling these things was okay. That's because I didn't understand the natural ebb and flow of the creative process. I thought every rejection meant I wasn't cut out to be a writer. I thought every late check meant my clients didn't respect me. I thought having a hard day meant I wasn't strong enough to hack it on my own.

All in all, I wasn't positive. I didn't know about the creative process that M.J. Ryan so eloquently discussed in Chapter 4. I was going with the flow, letting actions dictate my moods. So when I started thinking positively, I found that I could more easily cope with things like rejection. After all, it was only *one* rejection; it didn't mean that everyone hated my work. Time after time, I proved I could get clients and satisfy their professional needs. My worth didn't need to be tied up in one bad experience. By trial and error, I finally came to see that I was (and am!) a very good writer, and that the downs are just as much of this business as the ups. Even 9-to-5-ers have down times at their jobs. And for those who are miserable at those jobs, every day is down time.

My point is, in this special career path you have made for yourself, there are ups and downs. The highs hit high and the lows can bring you into the depths. There's no one else to hold you up until you build your own confidence and develop your support system. The tools to your success will ultimately lie in yourself. What I found was that it was okay that I wasn't born positive—I could learn how to enjoy this life even with all of its ups and downs. Having to stay positive with work spilled over into my personal life, and has made me a stronger, more mindful individual.

Beth Erickson, a writer mentioned in Chapter 1, had some very insightful things to say about staying positive. "The trick is to not focus on the negative. Negatives always exist. It's a reality we face," she says. The key word there is *focus*, because as I said, there will be inevitable downs. Erickson believes that when creatives focus on negatives, they actually wind up stifling their creative energy. This vigor is the very pinnacle of our success. For her, when that creative energy is zapped out, she faces writer's block, and that can produce anxiety and aggravation. "If you keep your mind focused on the positives going on in your life—and there are *always* positive things going on—you allow your creative juices to flow," she says. That, in turn, generates the creative energy freelancers need to *create*.

I like Erickson's message, and I think it sums up this chapter well. If you're like me and are getting ambushed by the slow times, try to practice some positive thinking. For example, evaluate your work. If you know it's good, *choose* not to let *one* rejection get in the way of your happiness. If you're in a rut and not getting a lot of projects in, do your best and trust the process. If you're feeling alone, realize that it's inevitable to feel a little abandoned, and then seek out support and friends to mingle with.

Dealing with the ups and downs of creative self-employment is all about taking action. How exactly do you do this? Gradually. That's the best advice I can give. I became stronger over time. I think the *biggest* part of success in this business is sticking with it. Those who can are the ones who inherit the strength to continue. It'll happen eventually, but no one says you can't speed up the process and put on your happy hat.

Do whatever it takes to give yourself the tools you need to succeed. If you have to take a trip down the self-help aisle and pick up a few Dr. Phil books, do it. If you need a life coach or therapist to get you on track, get one. You'll find that this career is about more than work; it is also about personal growth. Nurture yourself and your business will soar, too.

Finally, remember the ebb and flow. Don't get washed over *by* the waves, but do float *with* them. "It's all a cycle. You choose whether to dwell in the negative cycle or the positive one," says

Erickson. "It's a conscious choice daily. We have the freedom to choose however we want to live."

Challenges of Creative Self-Employment

ArLyne Diamond, Ph.D., is a management consultant and professional development coach based in California. She says there are four main challenges that creatives face: not having people to bounce ideas off of when they need them; staying on target and having the discipline to do what needs to be done when it has to be done; balancing marketing and networking time so creatives can be paid for their talents; and never knowing where or when the next contract is coming from. These challenges explain why many creatives face times of emotional difficulty. But is it only creative self-employment that can cause these issues?

"[Creative self-employment] is far more stressful in some ways than working for someone else," says Diamond, "Partially because you have to bring in the business and the money, and partially because you have to make all the decisions and can't merely conform and follow instructions."

Liz Bywater, Ph.D., says that self-employment has a different impact on different individuals. As the president of Bywater Consulting Group based in Pennsylvania, she consults with businesses about individual and organizational performance issues. She believes that the psychological challenges of creative self-employment include being able to tolerate uncertainty about finances and not grow extensively anxious or depressed; being able to structure one's lifestyle around self-employment; being able to reach out to others for support, encouragement and guidance; and being able to deal with feeling lonely, isolated and even depressed.

Challenges such as lack of financial security, benefits and camaraderie can cause more stress, but that can also be reduced due to other beneficial aspects of self-employment such as greater independence and flexibility. "Stress can be greater for the self-employed than others due to [these] factors, particularly the uncertainty about financial well-being," Bywater says. "Not having coworkers/colleagues to vent to and commiserate with can also add to stress. In addition, some individuals can become highly anxious and stressed by having to operate their own business without the external structure created by a workplace environment."

That's why Bywater emphasizes the importance of having a support network (which you will hear her talk about in Chapter 8) and doing your best to strike a healthy balance between work and the rest of your life. "You should be sure to have social activities, family time, self-care and physical activity scheduled into your week. Each day should have room for some departure from working," says Bywater. She says taking time to sit down to a healthy meal, getting dressed in the morning and taking care of yourself are key so you don't detracted from your sense of yourself as a vibrant, productive, successful business owner. "Believe you will be successful. Our thoughts lay the foundation for what we create and become."

CREATIVE PROFILE
ArLyne Diamond, Ph.D.
Consultant
Santa Clara, California

Creative Self-Employment Issues
"Loneliness, depression and even anxiety are common problems creatives can face when coping with creative self-employment," says ArLyne Diamond, who has an extensive career in business, education, psychology and consulting. "Being alone without stimulation, companionship and feedback from others can exacerbate whatever emotional tendencies you have. Also, not having someone else provide structure can and often does create 'existential anxiety.'"

Personal Work
ArLyne says that creative work is highly personal and therefore very attached to our sense of our selves and our egos. "In addition, in order to produce our best creative work we need to be emotionally open and available—thus more vulnerable," she adds.

Staying Balanced
"For me, and thus the advice I give others is to be sure to have social contact of both a personal and professional nature. For example, I spent last Sunday at a workshop with peers—I was one of the panelists—and I came away refreshed and revitalized. Balance means finding time to get what you need from the universe in the form of feedback, fun, support, ideas, love, exercise, etc."

For more information about ArLyne, visit www.diamondassociates.net.

CHAPTER 8

THE SUPPORT EDGE

While you cannot rely solely on other people to help you navigate the wild, untamed path of self-employment, there's nothing wrong with letting someone hold your hand along the way. Support is vital for most people, even for those who may not need the emotional benefits that come from support—they can use networking that a support system provides as a maintenance tool.

This chapter focuses on the various ways creatives develop their support systems. Whether you have to discipline yourself by managing your calendar or surround yourself with positive people, you'll hear various methods for getting the backing you need to thrive in your business, and you'll gain some insight into self-growth that will enable you to become your own support system.

Why Creatives Need Support

There's nothing wrong with seeking out support. In fact, it's quite necessary. Why? Because what we do as creatives is so unique. So different that it can feel like we're floating on a hammock without the intertwined rope beneath us. Point is, there is little support because we are all alone. Creatives need support in various ways some need socialization; others need someone to talk to about the issues they face as creatives.

People don't make it much easier on us. Some are envious and take their jealousy out on us. Others give us a hard time, thinking we can drop everything and tend to them because we don't have a set schedule. Those closest to us—*especially* those closest to us—can discourage us from pursuing our dreams the most, or at least make it difficult to do so.

Stephanie M. Cockerl, a Web consultant from New York City, said she struggles every month with various worries such as paying the rent, being able to afford medical insurance and getting the money she's owed by her clients. "Everyone thinks that I have such a sweet existence, but I don't," says Cockerl.

For example, she remembers a friend who most likely got upset after she bailed on a night out. She says she couldn't make it out because her creativity hit and she decided to go with the moment. "When creativity hits, I just cannot abandon it. I have to see it through," she explains. Few people would understand why one would break plans with a friend because they felt creative, but if you're reading this, you probably do. You may not have done the same, but Cockerl's story illustrates a point: Sometimes, as creatives, we do things that others may not comprehend. Some people may not understand our very existence as creatively self-employed workers. That's why it's important to institute a support system.

Note that I said *creating* a support system. Support systems don't generally come in neat, perfect little packages. Sometimes you have to make things work yourself. You created your own destiny when you plunged into creative self-employment, and you'll need to do the same to make sure you stay there.

Physical Support

Sometimes the best support system rests within. When Sandra Busta, a graphic designer and fine artist from California, was only 30 years old, her doctor told her to keep an eye on her heart. The stress had been affecting her physical health, and he warned that she needed take better care of herself to maintain her well-being. But for Busta, it wasn't easy to put her physical health first.

"I am a workaholic … and I need to be careful," she says. "I push myself too hard because I love my job, and because the demand is too high at times. It's hard dealing with deadlines." In response, she created a calendar to schedule time off for herself. She says she has to force herself to make time, but at least she's making it. I understand where she's coming from. Sometimes it's hard to pull away from work, especially on a crucial deadline. And when you don't have time to lean on others for support, it can feel like there is no one to help. But that's when you've got to learn to lean on yourself and learn how to best support yourself.

Jeff Fisher, an Oregon-based graphic designer specializing in business logos, knows what a physical toll work can take on one's health. At the age of 35, he experienced a variety of health issues. He wasn't able to sleep more than a couple of hours at a time, and was edgy. No surprise there—he was working 80 to 100 hours a week.

"I went to a doctor for a complete physical," recalls Fisher. "He checked my blood pressure three times, thinking that his equipment was broken. He finally sat me down and asked, 'What the hell is going on in your life?'" Fisher told the doctor all about his work, noting how one client was nearly 80 percent of his business. When that client said "jump!" Fisher says, he was "usually already in mid-air."

The doctor told Fisher that his blood pressure was higher than that of his father, who was on blood pressure medication; and that between stress and that family history, he was a heart attack just waiting to happen. "His prescription was to 'fire' the big, demanding client. The following week I did so, even though the thought of it made me even more ill," says Fisher. "Within a few weeks I made several new and interesting clients. I have not let work totally control my life since," he says. "I now work to live, not live to work."

When stress caused by creative self-employment takes a toll on your health, you may have to force yourself to take a break. Take a day off. Call in sick to your own voicemail and enjoy the carefree feeling that used to come with doing it to your boss. Think of it this way: If you can't physically function, your business will never prosper.

Looking Up for Support

Regardless of religion, many creatives find that spirituality has a hand in determining their success, and a big part of that is seeking support from their spiritual sides. For Nancy Ballew, a mural artist from Georgia, belonging to a women's prayer group helps. "I get lots of support from my friends in my spiritual community," says Ballew, who was laid off in 1991. After that, she did not wind up looking for full-time employment, and she's come to accept her talents as a muralist and her drive for self-employment.

"I need constant support in order to believe in myself and value what I do," says Ballew. But she's reached out and been able to find the support she needs to keep believing in herself and her business. For her, looking within is important, looking around is a stronghold, and looking up is a necessity. Regardless what you believe, your spirituality may be a wonderful tool for self-support and motivation.

Why Friends and Family May Not Be Enough

Susan Ariel Rainbow Kennedy (SARK), whom we met in Chapter 2 and again in Chapter 6, discusses the importance of support systems in her book *Make Your Creative Dreams REAL*. She makes a wise observation, saying that friends and family often are not aware of our creative dreams because those aspirations can be so personal.

That's true. Half of my family did not know I was writing this book until a few months before it went to print. Honestly, I didn't want to be bothered with all the excitement; I knew it would produce too much pressure to report back on every happening. If you do want friends and family to support you, it is wise to first select those people who make you feel most comfortable. For me, it was Tim who I first approached with the idea. He, of course, backed me throughout the entire process. I still think he's the only other person besides me who understands my passion for the concept of this book.

After you select people to support you, it's best to tell them *exactly* what you're looking for. SARK recommends letting them know you would appreciate no judgment during the process. If a person does not suit your support needs, let him or her know in a polite way that you do not need their support.

A practical way I found support was to turn to other creatives in my life. Invariably, they provided sound advice and a stable sounding board for me to vent about the project and discuss it. I trusted them instinctively because I *knew* that they *knew*. In fact, I've become friendly with many of the creatives in this book. Plenty of them were excited to be able to talk about their lives, and I was just as eager to bring the idea of creative self-employment into the spotlight. From there, many friendships have developed. There were, however, some colleagues who were *not* as supportive. I've found this to be very true if you use an Internet forum for support, depending which site you go to. As a result, I post general questions instead of exact details. Even still, I've found some creatives to be conceited and unpleasant. That's okay—the creatively self-employed are people, and not all people are pleasant. But there *are* people out there to support you; just take your time and find the right people or the right forum.

SARK recommends putting together a "Creative Dream Team" to get started. These groups can be valuable after you have started your self-employment as well. You may find that you've outgrown a group that got you started, which is completely normal. There are plenty of industry-specific networking groups to consider.

Then there is the most important support group: you, you and *you*. That's right. You can't always call on your imaginative chums for support at 3 a.m. when you're stuck on a paragraph or having another type of creative crisis. You have to be able to rely on yourself to get you through the struggles; the group is there to build you up so you can respond to trials when they come along. You deserve self-support; and quite frankly, you have to develop it to survive in the creative industry. There are no coworkers to meet for a water-cooler rant; it's just you. Build yourself up, and you'll see your business growing just as sturdy.

Pulling in the Positive

Part of becoming your own support system does not mean you have to be full of inner wisdom all the time. You just have to make a conscious decision to surround yourself with positive people. That's what Penny C. Sansevieri, an author who runs her own book marketing and publicity firm based in California, does. "I try to align myself with others who are self-employed because people who are in corporate America don't understand *truly* what it's like to be out on your own," she says. "I have been blessed with some very solid supporters, I don't know what I would have done without this fan club."

Sansevieri remembers starting out (with nothing in her savings account, remarkably), and being attentive to who she listened to, what she listened to and what she read. "I was super careful not to associate with nay-sayers," says Sansevieri. "In fact, I had an old boyfriend who at the time was trying to rekindle our relationship, during a dinner date one night he said to me, 'So, when are you going to quit this and get a real job?'" It was the last time she saw him.

"You have to be very careful what you let in when you're starting out. It's sort of like not watching a scary movie before you go to bed to fend off the nightmares. What you allow into your world becomes a part of you. If you let doubt in, either through your own self-talk or through the criticisms of other people, you'll fall into the trap of believing what you hear," she says. No wonder her business has been such a success. She not only has a physical support system of friends to help put things back into perspective when they stray, but she works towards her happiness proactively by focusing on— and only letting in—the good things in life. If you think supporting yourself is difficult, Sansevieri's method is a great way to get into the habit. Even if you cannot support yourself at first, surrounding yourself with positivity will give you a wonderful amount of strength.

How to Hold Yourself Up

There are many innovative, simple ways to create the support you need. Going to those you know is easiest for many, while others prefer to meet new creatives. You do not necessarily need to meet people in your exact career, either; a self-employed accountant friend, for example, may be able to give you valuable backing.

Some people say networking is the best way to meet other people, and I definitely agree. Remember that sometimes you have to feel out a professional organization to see if it will benefit you, but there are so many groups out there that can be a perfect fit. Then there's the Internet. With forums, chat rooms and other online communities, you can communicate easily with others. Many of this book's interviewees have blogs, or online journals, and use those to communicate. (Not familiar with blogs? Hit up www.six-apart.com, www.blogger.com or www.livejournal.com to see what they're all about.)

Even making a date to do something with a friend is supporting yourself. It's giving yourself a break and letting yourself rejuvenate. After all, support doesn't come focused only on your career. You can do non–business-related things and still feel supported. Some people don't need the heart-to-heart talk; some just need a break.

When it comes to self-support, I always found that taking time out for myself was key to gaining perspective and feeling revitalized. If there was no one to speak with when I was in a pinch, I could find the answers by clearing my head a little. Starbucks was an escape where I could work and relax at the same time. But then there were days when I needed a mini-vacation. For me, retail therapy worked. So did hitting the gym or heading to the beach. It was easy to dream of things I wanted to do—or not even think at all—with the time I had when I could take time off. For me, it was easier to do the enjoyable things when I was actually busy and had paying work coming in. Taking an afternoon off to shop when I had no projects coming in was harder. (And less practical, if you ask me.) The most difficult part about self-support, I think, is simply giving it to yourself.

Sometimes we need to give ourselves permission to take a break.

This is especially true for most of the creatives mentioned in this book. I'd say about 90 percent considered themselves workaholics—

workaholics who love what they do, but workaholics nonetheless. Workaholic or not, however you create your support system, *do* make one. "Having a support network is really important," says Liz Bywater, Ph.D., who was featured in Chapter 7. "Talking to others and seeing others regularly can combat loneliness and isolation. Having a financial back-up plan can reduce stress and anxiety as well. Being proactive about your business (even though it may also be your 'craft' or art) is important."

CREATIVE PROFILE
Jeff Fisher
Graphic Designer and Author
Portland, Oregon

Getting Started

Jeff Fisher has worked professionally as a graphic designer for more than 30 years. He is the author of the *Savvy Designer's Guide to Success: Ideas and Tactics for a Killer Career*. He has received over 500 regional, national and international design awards for his logo and corporate identity efforts.

Odd Man Out?

"As someone who gets a lot of public exposure, putting myself 'out there' personally has sometimes been a bit more difficult," says Jeff. After being let go from an ad agency about 20 years ago, his coworkers informed him that he was relieved of his job because the firm owner was "uncomfortable" having an openly gay employee. "I was stunned," says Jeff, who now enjoys plenty of successful business relationships.

"Being honest about my life, and exposing a very personal side, has allowed me to be much more creative [because] I have not allowed any restrictions to be placed on my work—by myself or others!"

Finding Support

About five years ago, Jeff helped form a group that held a weekly breakfast meeting. "It's turned into a weekly support group, as well as a reason to take a shower, get dressed and get out of the house," he says. "Other businesspeople pop in and out of the group, but the core group [of creatives] remains the same. The café owner refers to us as her 'weekly live entertainment.'"

To learn more about Jeff, visit www.jfisherlogomotives.com.

CHAPTER 9

✦

GOOD BUSINESS

True confession: I still do all of my accounting in a single Microsoft Excel spreadsheet. Tim continually hounds me to buy a super-nifty financial accounting program, but I can't bring myself to do it. I mean, at least I *have* a system. And although the accountant shrieks when she sees it each year, it works for me. The sad thing is, though, that my system is high-tech and advanced compared to those that some of you reading this use. That is, compared to the pile of hand-written invoices sitting in the corner of your room. (Please don't tell me you *really* have *handwritten* invoices tossed in the corner of your home office!)

My point is this: If you're running a business, you have to treat it like a business. And while my handy-dandy Excel sheet isn't break-ing ground, it *is* keeping me on top of invoices (which *are* profes-sional looking, and include my logo on top to be extra business-like).

I wrote this chapter to help you conduct good business. Most of this book offers comfort; this chapter offers advice. It's the closest thing to a how-to book that you're going to get from me. I'm the kind of person who doesn't believe in one way of doing things. Even so, you need to have some sort of professionalism. Many creatives don't; hence, why this chapter is here.

Despite all the worries and doubts that come with being a creatively self-employed worker, there are ways to combat them. Being a first-rate businessperson is one way. When your venture is professional and functioning well, it will grow. You won't have to worry about finding new clients or being uninspired. Those worries will be off your shoulders so you can move forward. That being said, it's often found that creative types could dress up an invoice with paint and embellishments much more easily than they could compile and organize the financial information to create one. Let's face it—we've got creative minds that have little room for crunching numbers and developing marketing plans. Those are areas for those with strong left brains. So what are the creative right-brainers to do when they have to incorporate good business practices in order to succeed in business for themselves? *Learn how to do it.*

Just as you take lessons when you want to learn how to draw or you take a course to improve your grammar, there are things that creatives need to learn in order to be in business—and there's nothing wrong with learning how to handle it. In fact, this is why big businesses hire creative consultants to help them compensate in the imaginative areas their business needs to thrive. Just so, we have to learn how to play the business game. You're dealing with big and small businesses that work professionally.

You cannot thrive on your creative talents if you do not have good business sense.

Most likely, if you're good at designing or creating, you are not a natural-born salesperson, or a marketer. You won't know how to promote your services or goods to others. But fear not! It is totally okay to be right-brained. The trick is in realizing that there are left-brained necessities that will help your business flourish. When they do not come naturally, it's okay—even smart—to take a few lessons.

Learn. I offer this answer because it's really all you *can* do to create a strong business. Chances are, you are not an entrepreneurial whiz; chances are, you never even took the time to create a business plan—you just took the time to *create*, and that's alright. But the most successful freelancers know that without solid business knowledge, a talent can only be a hobby, as opposed to a talent that they can make a living from.

Cashing in on Finances

For Christine Miller, whom we met in Chapter 4, counting on steady money always been a struggle. That's why she has to go out of her way to make time to arrange her finances. It may sound silly to be organized to the point of obsession, but for some freelancers, it's the only way to muddle through the sea of numbers.

"There has never been a time when my income has been consistent for more than a few months, and even when it has flowed in steadily, the arrival dates of checks, royalties and other receivables has always been something I have had to juggle," says Miller. "Even if I have a stack of checks due to me, I can never count on when they will arrive, so I always feel like I'm awkwardly maneuvering my way through the due dates of my bills."

To make sure she stay on top, she creates monthly budgets and checks in on them during the month. "I do not count on any check, advance, art purchase or anything else anyone promises me until I have the money in my hands. To me, it does not exist if it is not in my bank account," she says.

Most creatives have a fiscal tracking system and realize its importance. If you don't, you can start with something basic. Even an Excel spreadsheet is *something*!

For the Love of Lump Sums

A lot of creatives know how to stockpile money for the lean months. They also realize the joy of large checks because, unlike for most people, the self-employed creative knows that the money doesn't come regularly—but when a good project pays off, boy, does it *pay*.

Jackie Alpers, a fine art photographer and photo editor mentioned in Chapter 5, used to struggle with money as well. But her challenges came when she finally got the check: what to do, what to do? "When a big check came in I would want to spend it all right away. Then in couple of months I would be worried about paying my bills," says Alpers.

She's learned some restraint and budgeting techniques since the days of her newfound love of lump sums, but what's hardest is to have faith that the next check will arrive. "I've also learned not to worry about where the next check is going to come from," says Alpers, whose clients include Simon and Schuster, *Glamour* magazine and Canyon Ranch resort. "There's an unlimited source of income out there, and worrying isn't productive."

Of course it takes time to get to a well-established place with your creative business where you are getting regular work and not fretting about making enough money. It also takes time to learn how to manage your finances as a self-employed individual. It's completely okay for these things to take a while.

Taking What You Can Get

Earning secure money is not the only day-to-day business difficulty for creatives, but it's a popular gripe. Still, not getting enough of it is not the only complexity associated with the green. Angela Moore, who worked in the music industry for 16 years before starting Starfish Public Relations in California, says the hardest part of her business is knowing whether she's charging clients enough money.

"I am underpaid by most clients because I really want their business and do whatever it takes to get it," says Moore, who acknowledges that she takes on jobs free for friends and family because she loves her work so much.

Another struggle for Moore is when a client is dissatisfied with her work, which happened during her start-up years. "My partner (at the time) and I took any job we could to make money," she adds.

Now, Moore says she's in a position to take on clients that excite her, which provides her with engaging work initiatives that get outcomes. This way, she can put her all into the job and produce pleasing results for each customer. Her latest result is having succeeded enough to hire another employee. Though she will have to output more of her profit, she'll also get more patrons by taking on extra help. "No client is a long-term guarantee ... so I am always looking for new business. Hiring my new employee has enabled me to get more work," Moore says.

Riding the Collections Express

To make any self-employed business venture work, money always comes into play. For creatives, it can be hard to not only know how to invoice clients, or when to put your foot down when "the check is in the mail" yet never arrives. Time and time again, I've struggled with how to approach a client in various situations.

Even with credibility, it's tough to be harsh after 30 days has passed since the date of an invoice and I'm without the moohlah. *Should I send a polite e-mail? Should I call the accounting department? Should I go threaten never to work for the client again? Should I call a collections agency?* This is what goes through my head when I'm lacking the green.

After I talked to all of the creatives featured in this book, it looks like I'm not the only one who has struggled here. Even so, I find that many freelancers have to develop their own business practices and stick up for themselves when it comes to a client or project. Even though it's the hand that feeds you and you may lose a client, there will always be other sources of income if you manage your business correctly.

Von Glitschka, whom we met in Chapter 3, agrees that clients who are slow to pay have been his biggest obstacle. "This is basically the only area that I have trouble in from time to time. It's not all the time but enough that when it happens it's a major pain," Glitschka says. "Requiring half [of the payment] upfront has helped a bunch, but some agency clients just do not work that way. They pay good, but it's not very fast." After the politeness wears thin, Glitschka says, he has used a collection agency for clients who try to flake out. "Overall it's not a huge problem for me, but enough so to classify it as the worst part of running my own business."

Moore agrees, and admits that she has struggled to understand how some patrons go from constantly communicating with her when their project isn't finished to not responding to her inquiries for money owed. "[It] makes you want to cry," she says. "I worry about my reputation. I have to pick myself up and remind myself of the numerous other happy clients and redirect my energy in a positive way."

Because creatives can bill customers in different ways—by the hour, by the project, half up front, in full up front—it is important to develop a system of billing and collecting that works for you.

Logging Long Hours

Business can be rough when you are the only one raking in the cash—or trying to. That's why most self-employed creative types I interviewed confessed they were workaholics. "I love what I do; I can't stand to fail," says Phillis Stacy-Brooks, creative director of Main Street Graphics, her California-based company that specializes in Web design and branding. "When an idea comes to me, I'm right at the computer—even if it's 4 a.m.!" Stacy-Brooks knows that hours are hard to manage. She's not quite ready to hire office help, but says that handling all of the paperwork herself can be stressful. "I work way too much, but I do not believe that hinders my success," she says.

That all depends on the person. Sometimes, I'm completely wrapped up in something and enjoying myself. Most of those times are when I'm doing something personally interesting, or working with a client who has made my job easy. As a copywriter, I write for various companies. Admittedly, I can tell you I preferred working for a client of mine who launched a handbag line rather than trying to decipher the mysteries of mortgages for a financial firm.

But then there are times (usually when my plate is full and I'm not worrying about where the bacon will come from) when I want to gag at the very thought of writing. Still, I must come clean: I am a workaholic. Why? Because I'm always searching for new clients. Because you can't rely on every client to retain you. Because I want to make sure I have enough money.

But "why" the most?

Because I love what I do.

Self-Imposed High Standards

Matt Ramos, a photographer from New York, knows all about working long hours, but he says it's essential for freelancers to do so in order to stay on top of the game—and stay fed. "I feel not having the proper work ethic or working enough will greatly hinder your success in any business," he says. Ramos says that he can work upwards of 80 hours a week and lose sight of taking care of himself.

"I … find myself always pushing the limits to get as much done as possible, when I should probably be sleeping," says Ramos. "Believe it or not, I am harder on myself and own business than I would be if having a boss—the expectations of my own business are twice of anywhere else I could imagine."

But he knows how important balance is, and says he tries not to bite off more than he can chew so the quality of his work is not affected. Not only does Ramos shoot weddings, but he is responsible for photographing nationally known products and corporate executives. As he grows in his industry, he has been able to do so with great success because he takes his business super-seriously and never procrastinates. For Ramos, the secret is staying tough but remembering to find steadiness when you need it. Even if you have to "remind" yourself to make time for yourself, it is still essential to do so.

"Simply because I am somewhat of a high-stress person and perfectionist, I do not procrastinate when it comes to business," says Ramos. "An obligation to meet the client's needs in a timely fashion is always a priority."

Sounds like a lot of us work our tails off in a field where you sometimes really *do* have you work to gratify others. No wonder we can be just a *tad* sensitive about rejection. Still, pleasing clients is imperative to your success, and Ramos' suggestion is a great way to make customer satisfaction as painless as possible. Let's look at another way to work *with* your clientele.

Keeping Clients Happy

Ruth Clare is another creative freelancer who owns up to struggling with keeping clients satisfied and meeting her individual business needs. The copywriter works side by side with her husband, and the two run Mono Design, based in Australia. But even Down Under, she says, she has to come up with arrangements that work for her and fulfill the client's needs, too, and that can be a balancing act. She says the pull between figuring out how much to charge, guessing how much is possible for the clients' budgets, determining how long a project will take—*and* managing expectations—is the hardest thing about being in business.

What has helped her is educating clients as much as possible about how her work process operates, how her services can make them—and *save* them—money, and what they can do to keep her costs down. She says that clearly defining the working partnership at the start of it helps save time and money as well, and it makes for a smoother relationship. "I spend a lot of time at the beginning of the process getting clear about their specific goals for any piece of communication we are producing so we can both keep our attention focused on those," Clare says.

It is vital to communicate with your clients (even when they don't reciprocate as well). I can't stress this enough. Not only will you have more of a chance of pinpointing their needs and creating to their satisfaction, but you'll be more likely to retain the patron.

Getting It in Writing

From the get-go of my business, I knew to have a contract. After researching other copywriters' websites, I had a gist that it was important to protect my rights. I drew up a standard contract, which I use to this day on every project—even when the client seems trustworthy, and even when they give me a retainer up front. Why? Because I'm a businesswoman—and a smart one.

So is Cat Morley, a designer and project manager based in Thailand. In addition to running www.creativelatitude.com, a hub for creatives, she is the owner Katzi Design. She says contracts are a way of life. "When I was starting out, I wasn't as skilled in designer–client communication. As a result, there were some snafus," she recalls. "But, after you've wasted your time because you didn't cover your hind quarter, you quickly search out ways to combat the problem."

See? Another trial-and-error situation. But if you don't have a contract to start with—right now—look into it. I promise it will save you sweat, help you make sure you get paid, give you clearly defined rights to your work and help you keep client relationships running smoothly. Morley also reminds creatives to keep open communication with customers, especially when project specs change. If something along the way deviates from what was originally agreed upon, creatives need to go back and clarify in the new expectations in writing or risk rejection and even losing the client. She's right: Communicate—and do it in writing.

How Much Are You Worth?

When you're the boss, how do you know what rules to set? With the amount of freedom freelancers have, it's easy for many to give themselves a long coffee break during the day. But when it comes down to business, you have to know the industry to play with the big boys.

Andrew Hindes, a copywriter from California, had some corporate experience before breaking off on his own. But there were still standards to set for himself, one of which was pricing. "It's something that somehow hasn't gotten much easier even though I've done a lot of bids, probably because every project and every client is different," says Hindes, who says that he also fears not getting another assignment each time he receives one. Though the jobs keep coming in, he continues to struggle to keep his prices consistent.

In an industry where you can make a fat hourly wage or a nice lump sum for completing a project, it's hard for some freelancers to set their own standards. When I started as a writer, I made it a priority to work at an affordable rate, probably one that was way too inexpensive. So as time went on and I saw what I could be making, I naturally was inclined to raise my prices. However, I've still kept my rates reasonably priced. It's what I've built my business motto on. ("Your words are worth a lot. Mine only cost a little.")

But it's not easy to maintain low prices when you see others charging more for services. Many freelancers struggle to define what they're worth in a dollar amount. Thank goodness for resources that give freelancers ranges of rates for common types of projects and services to use as guidelines. Obviously those just starting out in writing, for example, do not mind writing at $0.10 a word, but veterans demand—and deserve—a few bucks a word. When I investigated copywriting rates, I found that others in my field could earn $30, $50—even $100—an hour. Knowing I didn't have as much experience as those who were charging on the higher end, I started with lower rates. I still charge on the low- to mid-range side of the spectrum. Not only because I feel charging more would be a rip-off; but because I want to keep things reasonably priced for my clients.

As time goes on, many creatives find that they settle at a price range they feel they're worth; and as their experience grows, they can make a very good living. For Hindes, who has built up his clientele, he's now confident that his self-employment can support his family. Now it's on to building up for retirement and funding education for his children. But he finds that as a writer settled into his career, he doesn't really need to worry about never finding another assignment—they keep coming along, so he must be doing something right.

Defining "Work"

Lain Ehmann, a writer from California, says creatives have to be careful how they define work. "A broad definition could find you 'working' all the time, but making little progress. On the other side of the coin, a narrow definition means you only count it as 'work' if you are getting paid for it," she explains. All the same, I would say you're still working if you're marketing yourself. Those payoffs won't be instant—but new work comes from it!

Like most of us, she has found that she doesn't have to work eight hours a day to make a living. On a per-hour basis, she can earn more because she works more productively and is compensated based on what she produces instead of how many hours she spends in an office. Still, she says it is easy to get wrapped up in "work" when she's not really working. "I find I can read tons of books on my topic, cruise the Internet all day, chat with like-minded friends, all under the guise of working," she says. "But at the end of the day, you have to sit down and do it [the actual client work]."

She raises a good point. As many writers know, when you spend all day in front of a computer, it's easy to let your mouse wander over to Internet Explorer or Firefox, which for some of us, inevitably leads to game playing, chatting or, say, an afternoon eBay spree. I'll be the first to admit that my online breaks have interrupted my working patterns, so I do my best to work and take breaks in separate blocks. Speaking of breaks, they're essential. Actually, *not* working 40 hours a week is a requirement for some.

Angela Mattson, a copywriter from North Carolina, is able to take four to five weeks of vacation per year. "I actually feel that working too *much* hinders my success," she says. "When I am trying to focus on too many projects at once, I start making mistakes or letting details slip through the cracks." If you can, take breaks. An actual vacation, an afternoon off or even five minutes for a cup of tea will help you recharge. Depending on the person, you *need* time off when you work as intensely as most of us do.

Mattson also brings up a personal factor about time that's worth mentioning. Even though most of our corporate friends don't understand us, that doesn't mean we should toss our freedom in their faces; most likely, they're envious of it. "I am careful not to gloat or talk too much about my freedom and success with my friends who *are* in the corporate world," she says.

That's a useful tip. Some people don't *get* how necessary these breaks are, or why you need to move your office outside on a sunny afternoon. Most of us do it not only because we *can*, but because we *thrive* on the inspiration. And while you should relish and enjoy the freedoms of self-employment that you deserve, rubbing it in that you took a spontaneous afternoon off may not be the best idea if you don't want to get some backlash from those not fortunate enough to do so. Of course, those who are true friends will not be upset if you share the perks of your job—if they do, you can ask them what it's like to have matching contributions in their 401(k). Better yet, ask them what it's like to have a 401(k) at all!

When It's Okay to Say "No"

When you've worked so hard to get clients, it can also be pretty ironic and confusing the first time you turn down work. If this has not yet happened to you, prepare for it. As your business grows, you may weed out customers who are not enjoyable to work with, or clients who do not pay as well as others. It may sound far off, but turning down work is quite common for successful freelancers.

Liz Kalloch, previously mentioned in Chapter 7, has gotten to that point. "I tend to say yes to everything and then stress myself out with the workload," she says. "I think sometimes that working too much hinders me." Kalloch says that working too much doesn't give her the time to get new kinds of design work and add to her illustration portfolio. She has been so busy with her print work that she has not had time in years to get multimedia design projects, websites and video work. That's why she says she is learning to say no if she's too busy and not give in to the fear that customers will never call her again for another job.

Her story reminds me of how I've felt in the past: the constant worry about losing a client when all along I know I should have faith, the guilt when I do turn down a job … it is all so challenging to deal with sometimes. But it's important to note that it *is*, in fact, okay to say no. When your physical health is in jeopardy, when your stress levels are too high, when a business relationship is toxic, it's not only okay to say no—it's *good* for you. It is most certainly a sign of growth; of that confident freelancer you dreamed of becoming after reading chapters 3 and 4.

You would think that with so much work, there's no way Kalloch is a procrastinator. Not so. "I find that the times that I do procrastinate are when I have taken too much work, and don't have the time to really focus on ideas, and direction and etc.," she says. "My mind will drift and I wander around the house trying to keep myself inspired, but often get nothing done."

Hearing Kalloch talk reminded me that even when you "make it" there can still be difficulties and struggles. Just knowing that it happens to others may help you if you go through similar situations.

When Clients Don't Play Fair

Kalloch had another story that was certainly worth mentioning, because you probably have a "bad client" story of your own to share. You know, the kind of situation when the check is supposedly in the mail but never shows up until you hire a collections agency, or the customer leads you on for weeks without replying, or the says they'll call and then fails to do so. The list is kind of endless—and clients can be pretty sleazy. Kalloch dealt with a particularly sleazy one.

She says she designed a line of cards for a rather large company. After being approved along the way, the final designs were together but the client said they didn't like them. Worse, Kalloch was told they were hiring someone else to redesign them—a*nd* they said they wouldn't pay her. "I thought long and hard about what to do," says Kalloch. "It was not a ton of money, but there was a principle involved for me, and in the long run I decided that it wasn't worth it." *What?* I thought when I read her story. Wait, it gets better.

Two years later, Kalloch says she was at a friend's birthday party and someone gave him one of the cards *she* designed. "There were no changes to it," she says. "I was so angry. I can still remember sitting across the room talking to someone, and glancing up as he was reading the card, and I could see the artwork on the front, and I was shocked, my mouth literally hung open."

It was then that Kalloch *did* take action. She wrote the company a letter about what was done. She says she never heard back from them. "I still see the cards in stores sometimes, and growl to myself," she says. "People who are going to 'steal' other people's valuable time, and people who are going to stiff you on a bill are out there. You can sign contracts, you can ask around about a new client to see if anyone has heard anything good or bad … you can do your best to make good decisions about who you work with and still you can get ripped off. It is a horrible pit-of-the-stomach, wrenching-your-insides-around-and-stirring-them-up kind of feeling."

So yes, bad clients happen. I didn't want to dwell on stories like these as to keep the book mostly positive; but like other aspects of creative living, I wanted to note it to remind you that you are *not* alone when you deal with something like this. Most likely, you will.

Succeeding With Marketing

While painting or writing may be easy for creatives, learning how to market and sell their creations or services can be difficult, as can keeping up with menial tasks, such as keeping track of invoices and filing. To make a creative business work, Patrick Snow, an author, speaker and coach from Washington, recommends that freelancers either learn how to market and run their businesses, or hire someone to handle the tedious, left-brained tasks. "The 'why' in self employment has to be so strong that it can and will overcome any lack of 'how,'" says Snow.

Zohar Adner, a certified empowerment coach from New York, agrees. "Learning the marketing/sales side of a business can be extremely taxing, time consuming and stressful," he says, but according to him, it's still a necessary evil for creatives to make business prosper. He says that the toughest part of learning how conduct left-brained business tasks is to analyze one's learning curve and continually reassess individual business expectations as time goes on.

Kelly James-Enger, a freelance journalist, author and motivational speaker, says creatives have to be careful not to blame their business-minded weaknesses on their personalities. As an Illinois-based consultant to corporations and other organizations, she meets people who are squeamish about marketing all the time.

Right or left brained, she believes there are no excuses when it comes to creatives learning how to market—they just *have* to. "Anyone can learn to use both the left and right halves of their brain," says James-Enger. "I'm not saying it's fun to do things that don't come naturally, but if you want to succeed as a self-employed person, that comes with the territory." In other words, as James-Enger says, "Suck it up, and do it." Sure, it's the tough-love approach to marketing, but it's the truth.

Art Javid, who, along with his brother Kevin, runs GraphicWise, a California-based graphic design firm, says facilitating new business is certainly the hardest part of creative self-employment. Marketing isn't a strong point for him or his brother, nor is it a desirable task. They'd rather just *create*, like most of us.

"As graphic designers, we tend to think that our talents alone will make for a successful business," says Javid. "Although that may be true for the most part, the other half of the equation is having to constantly find new business to keep our business afloat." That's why the brothers put aside at least one day a week to devote to marketing. "[We] pursue leads, do cold calls, or go to chamber of commerce meetings and sell ourselves to those who don't see the value of designers," Javid says.

So, how exactly do you promote yourself and your talents?

The Three Most Effective (and Inexpensive) Marketing Tools

Ilese Benun knows all about marketing—she's built a business on it. The New Jersey–based marketing consultant has authored four books and helps businesses of all kinds market their services. Because she's both a creative and a professional marketer, I was eager for her to share her knowledge with you. It's not that I don't think creatives know what we're doing, but this is a vital area of businesses that many of us clueless about, and rightfully so. Most people who can create are not as talented at the hard-wired, left-brain kind of stuff. As I've said, it's nothing to worry about—it just means that you have to *learn* how to market.

With so many promotional tools available, it can be overwhelming to decide which one or ones you may want to use in your business. Should you advertise? Build a website? Start an e-mail marketing campaign? Make some cold calls? Send a postcard to prospects? Attend a chamber of commerce meeting? According to

Benun, there are three ways the creatively self-employed can effectively and affordably market themselves:

- **Expand your universe with networking**. "There are tons of networking events to attend—too many, actually," says Benun. "Too many ways to meet people you'll never see again. Too many opportunities to collect a stack of business cards you'll never look at again." She reminds creatives that networking isn't a contest to see how many people you can meet. It's not even about schmoozing. It's simply the process of getting to know people over time and nurturing those relationships, she says.

    "You never know who will need what when," says Benun, who encourages creatives to find one or two groups where prospects gather. "Get involved and let them get to know you over time. Extend your hand and introduce yourself. Contribute to your community. Join the board of your local library or volunteer to organize a bake sale at a local school. Be visible."

- **Keep in touch regularly.** "The only way to stay in touch with everyone who's expressed interest in your work is with a regular marketing vehicle—what I call a 'loop'—something you do like clockwork, quarterly or even monthly, so you don't have to reinvent the marketing wheel each time," she says. Sending out a simple e-mail newsletter is the easiest and least expensive loop. (Don't worry, she adds, e-mail marketing is not the same thing as spam.) E-mail is one of the best and least expensive ways to keep in touch with—and keep your name in front of—those with whom you have (or would like to have) a working partnership. This includes past, current and possibly future customers, as well as vendors and colleagues and even friends and family. These people want to hear from you. Let them.

"An e-mail marketing campaign accomplishes many things at once," Benun says. Not only is it the ideal medium to showcase your work, share your knowledge and build credibility, while also spreading the word about your services and distinguishing you from others just like you, but it also drives traffic to your website in a more reliable and controllable way than you get from search engines. And it serves as a prompt for your recipients to touch base. When they get a message from you, it encourages them to respond.

I've gotten about 90 percent of my clients using this method. I'm assertive, I'm not afraid of a nasty reply (though I have *never* gotten one) and I have nothing to lose using this tactic. In fact, I agreed with this method so strongly that I called on copywriting guru Bob Bly to give creatives some tips on how to craft an e-mail marketing message. Read more about it at the end of this chapter.

- **Launch a website.** "These days, it's just plain unprofessional to say, 'I don't have a website,'" says Benun. It's almost like saying you don't have an answering machine, e-mail or voicemail. There's really no excuse. At the very least, you should have a one-page site with a blurb about your work and contact information. Later, you can develop a more multifaceted website with examples of your work, descriptions of the various services you offer and glowing testimonials from clients. You can also create a resource-rich site that positions you as an authority in your field and draws traffic. "Either way, having a website establishes you as a legitimate business," Benun says. "Even customers looking for local services go to the Web to check them out before they pick up the phone."

The Industry Learning Curve

After you market your services properly, you sort of become an expert in your field. You'll find people looking to *you* for help on getting into the biz, and tips for making it work. Laurie Barrows, a children's book illustrator and fine artist from California, was part of a networking group that gave her wonderful support as she began her career. It taught her a lot about how to improve her business marketing and run her company more effectively. She eventually outgrew the group, but says that was a good thing.

Now she's doing her part as a mentor to other artists, which at times can be frustrating. She gets irritated by emerging creatives who don't have a professional attitude and don't know about their industry or what it means to have poor business ethics. "Most of the artists I help mentor are great and have a thirst for learning about the field," she says. "There are those, however, who aren't willing to pay their dues, who think success will come overnight and can't handle rejection."

Sharon McCormick, a career coach based in Florida, says creatives need to learn about what she refers to as their occupational preferences. "Like being right-handed or left-handed, we are talented in different ways," she explains. "If I need talent that I don't have, I don't hesitate to call and hire someone who is an expert in their field. I outsource what I am not talented in so I can focus more on what I am talented in." Although McCormick is a strong advocate for nourishing creative talents, her insight into hiring out for help is a great idea. There is nothing wrong with using an accountant if you're no good with numbers.

Who knows, with a little networking, you could even swap services with that accountant who needs new website design or marketing materials! This is why it's important to learn everything you can, even heed the advice of a mentor or use a specialist, to build your business strong—because, it *is* a business.

The Impact of Your Business

For me, I didn't realize I was running a full-on business until I was browsing the printer section in a computer store one day with my husband. I ran my hand down the top of a gorgeous HP model, very impressed. This sucker did it all: faxed, printed photos, photocopied, scanned.

"One day," I motioned to my husband, who glanced at the deluxe mother-of-all printers.

"Actually, honey, you need something like that *now*," he said.

I glanced back in confusion. I had a printer. He had a scanner. Let us not mention the archaic fax machine I was using at the time … it was one of those one-page-at-a-time messes, sending but never receiving.

"No …" I looked away and continued walking down the aisle. The printers all got cheaper the farther I walked, so I assumed the object of my affection was the top-of-the-line model.

"Yes, you do," he continued behind me, stopping to examine the tag next to it to look at all of the features. "You do have a business, and you need to treat it like one."

I bought that puppy a few months later when my fax machine crapped out. I could have gone for another cheapie, but I wanted to invest in something better this time around. I needed a superior machine with the amount of faxing and printing I did. Not only that, but it was okay to splurge—I was a business, and it was a practical business expense. (That, and it would be a luxury to receive faxes, too!)

I'm not saying you should go out tomorrow and buy a couple thousand dollars worth of hardcore, state-of-the-art office equipment to pimp out your office—er, spare bedroom—but you have to take your business, and your investments in it, seriously. From equipment and your business materials to how you market yourself *and* work with clients—you've got to have a professional edge.

Taking Your Business to the Next Level

Professionalism is an imperative factor of creative self-employment that Peter Bowerman, a top author in the writing field, and I agree on very strongly. "This is a hard business in terms of getting yourself off the ground, but it's so worth it once you do," said Bowerman, whose books *The Well-Fed Writer, Back for Seconds: A Companion Volume to The Well-Fed Writer* and *The Well-Fed Self-Publisher: How to Turn One Book into a Full-Time Living* have given thousands of writers inspiration and ideas to properly market themselves. One of Bowerman's strong points is teaching writers exactly how to promote themselves, but many writers can be reluctant to learn. He finds that they are not only intimidated by creating marketing materials and business plans and reaching out for work instead of waiting for it to come; many do not know that it *is* necessary to excel in their businesses.

Let me say this: Marketing isn't hard. It's not rocket science. It is, simply enough, the art of putting yourself out there in a qualified way to garner new business and maintain existing clients. Whether you approach companies with your resume or portfolio, pass out fliers or attend a networking meeting, marketing doesn't offer an instant pay-off—but boy, it does pay off eventually! The best part is hearing out of the blue about a lead you generated ages ago. For example, I'll get calls even *years* after I sent my resume to a company asking to help with their corporate writing projects. When calls like that come in, it feels wonderful! One, because the marketing efforts do come back to you in time, and two, because every time you take time to promote yourself, it's like scattering seeds *everywhere* that can sprout into *anything* at any *time*!

Bowerman agrees that marketing is a must for any creative; otherwise, they will not make a living off their talents. That's okay if you're not *trying* to make your livelihood as a self-employed creative, but you're likely reading this book to learn how to survive on your creative talents. "The reason why a lot of creatives have a problem with treating their business like a business is because they've equated marketing as something difficult, that they're not good at, that they don't want to do," says Bowerman. "In this day and age, if you want to survive as a creative person, you have to be able to do more than just create." That's why Bowerman offers a straightforward approach to landing clients and running a business. He incorporates into the mix ideas such as making sales calls and approaching customers.

After reading Bowerman's second book, *Back for Seconds*, I realized something of my own: I didn't really learn a lot from it, I just realized I was on the right track. Here I was, sending direct-marketing materials out to businesses just has he recommended—and it was working. I recognized that I had a natural knack for pulling in clients. Not everyone is going to luck out with marketing like I did, and I'm here to tell you that it's okay. But you have to understand how important it is to take your business seriously, and put in a good effort to learn how to run it professionally.

What's helped me run a proficient business? Here are a few of my tricks:

- I approach clients I like, and don't rely on job openings for work

- I do what I'm good at (copywriting) to help pay the bills while I pursue "fun things" like magazine and book writing, which don't immediately pay off

- I make appointments and keep them

- I travel with a portfolio in my car

- I use a standard contract that shows I mean business

- I have a professional website and brochure, and business cards to match

- I devote hours every week just to marketing

- I set deadlines for myself and keep them

- I work to satisfy my clients' needs

- I send invoices to customers and require prompt payment

- I follow up with established and inactive clients using direct mail postcards

- I return phone calls and e-mails within 24 hours

- I am part of a professional organization

- I keep regular hours each day in my home office

- I schedule the majority of my work hours around the my peak productivity times during the day

There is no right or wrong way to market yourself, but professionalism must come into play. Bowerman notes that it is more of an *attitude* than an *aptitude* when it comes to succeeding in the business. There is not a single plan that works for everyone. "It's more about things you have to do than a way you have to be," he explains. Again, I agree. Plus, half the fun of being in a creative business is learning to do things in your own way—but you have to *do something*. If you're not a natural at marketing, that's not a problem. Even I need help (and enjoy) learning how to improve and grow my business. That is why I urge you to learn about business principles. And as you'll see in the next section, it's rather inexpensive to become a pro in no time.

Resources for Learning

Books and websites have taught me the most about running a successful, and serious, writing business. In my industry, folks like Bly and Bowerman have made a living writing books to help people like *me* succeed. These books include tips on how to market yourself, increase sales, retain customers and drum up new business. The tactics are usually very simple

For less than $20 a pop, I have learned a ton of simple ways to better my business. (Plug: Use your local library. They have dozens of books you can use to get ideas, and access to dozens more through inter-library loan programs. That and the reading list in Appendix B are sure to help you!) In addition, the Web is a valuable medium for information—and many of its resources are free. I've listed some valuable marketing websites in Appendix A. So now you know how important it is to get in the game and play with the major leagues. What are you waiting for?

Get off the bench!

MARKETING VIA E-MAIL

I've found Internet marketing to be *the* most valuable marketing tactic. Whether you're selling artwork or your editing services, you can reach people effectively by offering your services in a simple e-mail. But *do* be careful how you craft that message—these days, spam is on everyone's mind, and it can be hard to sort through an overflowing inbox.

Here are some tips for how to craft an effective marketing e-mail, excerpted from Bob Bly's article "15 Tips For Writing Internet Direct Mail That Works." I've added some of my own ideas in as well.

- Don't use "free" in the subject line. This is used in traditional direct marketing, but spam filters may pick it up in an e-mail. Make your subject line as personal as possible, perhaps by including the recipient's name or company.

- Use an attention-getting headline or lead-in sentence. Include an offer and response opportunity up top to grab the attention of readers who may be short on time. In the first paragraph, deliver a mini-version of your complete message. State the offer and provide an immediate response mechanism, such as clicking on a link connected to a Web page. These appeals to online prospects with short attention spans.

- Expand after the first paragraph to cover features, benefits and other details. This will appeal to the prospect who wants more information.

- Include another offer and response opportunity at the end of the message, and include a direct link to the applicable website, if possible. Limit the number of click-through links in the message to about three.

Continued on next page.

MORE MARKETING VIA E-MAIL

- Avoid weird wraps or breaks by using wide margins.

- Ease up on the all-caps function. You can use WORDS IN ALL CAPS but remember that the world of e-mail, all caps give the impression that you're shouting.

- In general, a shorter message is better.

- Try not to use too many graphics, or none at all.

- Write in a helpful, friendly, informative and educational tone—not a promotional or hard-sell tone. Use thoughtful phrases, and be specific. Why are you the best service? What do you have that other similar services do not?

- Include an opt-out statement for recipients who feel they have been spammed by stating that your intention is to respect their privacy, and making it easy for them to prevent further promotional e-mails from being sent to them. All they have to do is reply and type "UNSUBSCRIBE" or "REMOVE" in the subject line.

Find more great marketing writing tips at www.bly.com.

CREATIVE PROFILE
Patrick Snow
Author, Speaker and Coach
Bainbridge Island, Washington

Meeting Success

Patrick Snow is author of *Creating Your Own Destiny: How to Get Exactly What You Want Out of Life,* which has sold over 100,000 copies since first being published in 2001. In addition to writing other books, he has been featured in *USA Today* and *The New York Times,* and been featured as a guest on more than 350 radio stations throughout North America and Europe.

How Creatives Can Build Business

"The first thing one must do is completely learn to believe in oneself and eliminate all self doubts," says Patrick. If money is not coming in or the business is still building up, he recommends getting a part-time job to pay the bills while business increases.

Marketing vs. Advertising

Many freelancers consider advertising when growing their business, and also focus on marketing work. Snow says a successful business is five percent building or creating the product or service, and then 95 percent marketing the product or the service.

"The best way to get your work out there is to focus your efforts on marketing, not on advertising. Advertising is expensive and oftentimes does not work," Patrick says. "Marketing, on the other hand, is much less expensive and oftentimes works much better."

For more information about Patrick, visit
www.createyourowndestiny.com.

CHAPTER 10

✦

CREATIVELY SHINING

When I began receiving completed questionnaires from the interviewees for this book, everyone had a story to share. Most people had a lot of the same answers about the various creative self-employment aspects you've read about in this book: They like the freedom; they miss their steady paychecks; they're lonely, but fulfilled. And they all had at least one special memory to share about a time when they feel they creatively shined.

Many people said that just hearing a client sing their praises did wonderful things for their morale. Others had a moment when they realized that they had *arrived* in their respective industry. Even I told you about my epiphany in picking out an upscale fax/copier/printer/scanner, and about the first time I ventured to Starbucks to work in the middle of the day. These large and little delights are personal to each of us, and regardless of when it "clicks," it's wonderful.

The truth is that many of us relish our jobs. But we can get bogged down trying to handle administrative tasks, battle the lonelies, deal with rejection and work with clients. That is why it's important to go back to your roots sometimes; and for many of us that means remembering moments when we creatively excelled.

I wanted to briefly share some stories from creatives who have achieved great things large and small. My hope is that you will cling to your creatively shining moments and recall them if you get down in the dumps. I promise that if you look back at your achievements, it will help propel you to get ahead. A few interviewees had magical moments to share about a time when they shined. Let's hear a few.

Making Another's Success Your Own

Public relations began as a side job for Mike Farley, a musician living in Ohio. But in 2003, he headed to Nashville, Tennessee, to pursue songwriting opportunities like plenty of other artists who came before him. He has not gotten his big break quite yet as a musician. Instead, what was just a side job has taken off in a huge way—*huge* because Farley not only gets to handle public relations, but he does it for singer–songwriters who are now making it big. "I love it," says Farley of his work. "I never want to go back to the 9-to-5 corporate world ... ever."

That's because the rewards of Farley's jobs have allowed him to find a new calling. He can use his skills and experience to propel artists into the spotlight. While still working on his own career, Farley has built a network that one day may help him—and for now he's satisfied just helping others. Take Kate Voegele, a singer–songwriter from Cleveland. She's just one of Farley's works of art—a performer he buzzed about so much that she wound up getting a management deal and showcasing for every major label. Voegele has performed at Farm Aid the last two years, and won the USA Songwriting Competition. "While her talent earned her a lot of the success, we helped to launch her career and I'm proud of what we've done for her," says Farley.

That's what keeps him going; succeeding in a career he never thought would be profitable enough to support him and his wife,

Jen. She now works alongside him, and the two have a flourishing and enjoyable work environment. "She always believed in me and still does, and is a big reason we've been so successful," Farley says.

Helping Others

For Melanie Negrin, a copywriter featured in Chapter 1, her immaculate moment came when she won first place in the New Jersey Kiwanis Club Bulletin Contest. As a member of Kiwanis, an international community service organization, she used her marketing experience to help keep club members up to date on happenings through creation of its newsletter.

Negrin, who specializes in marketing communications for entrepreneurial businesses and non-profit organizations, had received numerous accolades from club members on the newsletter. But when she won the state competition, which put her in the running for the international award, she was even more proud of her efforts. She was later honored as Kiwanian of the Year by her home club and says it was a "truly incredible feeling."

Marisa Haedike, whom you also may remember from Chapter 1, may not think she's making much of an impact as she creates vibrant works of art that are displayed on her website, www.creativethursday.com. She named the site after the one day a week she made time to be creative when she was still working in a 9-to-5 job. When I ventured to her site, I was amazed at her talent. Not only was her artwork gorgeous, but she created a line of podcasts about creative living that really hit home for me. Haedike's podcasts cover everything about creative living: comparing ourselves to others, how to know when you're done with a creative project, meeting other creatives and beating perfectionism.

"This is truly the work I've loved the most," she says. "To know that my voice is resonating with people all over the world, that my art is inspiring them is especially great! It's just icing on the cake of doing work I love."

I was touched by her podcasts because they explored the intricacies of creative living. She adds a message to her collection each week, so you may want to subscribe to these free offerings for some ongoing support and enlightenment. It helped to hear another creative voice that I could relate to 110 percent.

Accidental Success

Sometimes our brightest moments come when we least expect them. For Monica Lee, whom we heard from in Chapter 5, it took a nasty bout with the flu for her to realize that she was on her mark. She was nearly done with an agreeable children's illustration job when she suddenly fell ill. Quickly, she worked to complete the job. Her husband lent a hand and drove her to FedEx to ship off the final art in order to make deadline.

"Where's the shiny part?" jokes Lee. "When I look at the work now I can't believe I finished in a feverish haze and it looks good! Instinct must have kicked in!"

There was Lee, down but not out with an illness that may have caused any other freelancer to take the afternoon off and call in with an excuse for missing the deadline ... but she stayed on track and did some of her best work innately. Even when she wasn't all there, her work was, proving that she is indeed a talented artist.

Something similar happened to Michelle Ponto, who shared some of her experiences in Chapter 7. When she applied on a whim to a film production house, claiming that she could write a script, she couldn't believe what happened. "They called me and said, 'Okay, here's the idea. You have two weeks to write the entire movie. Go!'" recalls Ponto. "Needless to say, I didn't sleep that night. This was the chance of a lifetime, but I had no idea if I could actually pull it off."

But two weeks later, she mailed the finished script to the production team—and they loved it. "Being under pressure, but knowing I would hate myself if I didn't do it, was the fire I needed to get my butt in gear and overcome my fear of failure," says Ponto. The films were in production at the time of this publication.

A Rewarding Career

For Chris Tomlinson, a graphic designer whom we met in Chapter 3, his proudest moment came when he completed a photo restoration project. The customer had brought in her wedding snapshot, which was one of the first color photos ever taken in his area. The picture was beaten up, tattered and discolored—but Tomlinson gave it his all and poured his heart into the restoration. The result? Rewards beyond what he could have imagined.

"When she arrived to pick up the photo, a tear rolled down her face as she looked at the photo. Her husband had passed many years prior to this restoration, and I believe we helped her remember a truly great time in her life by bringing the photo back to life," said Tomlinson. That's when work makes you feel really good—when you can make a difference in someone's days through your passion.

Amy Mantione, a graphic designer introduced in Chapter 7, helps a chapter of the Boys and Girls Club with a calendar that the organization sells at its annual gala benefit and throughout the year. "It is always so appreciated by the Board of Directors and the people that attend the gala," she says. "I have received compliments too numerous to mention, which always feels good, but at the same time, it is helping them generate revenue for their club, so I know that from a marketing perspective it was a successful piece."

What's in a Name? Plenty!

It also feels good to know that you are actively competing with the big firms. That's what happened to Art and Kevin Javid, the two brothers who run a graphic design business mentioned in Chapter 9. They left the 9-to-5 world knowing that the sooner they could break into creative self-employment, the sooner they could succeed. "We both felt guilty working at a 9-to-5 job because our long-range success ultimately depended on working for ourselves, and the longer we put it off, the longer it was going to take us to get where we wanted to be," says Art Javid. They broke free and never turned back.

The brothers were later on the phone with the director of marketing for a Fortune 500 company they did some design work for. He told them that it took the company 20 years to get to where the brothers were, and that was after hiring an in-house design team to help. "The CEO and president of that company were also in the room, and they both took turns to thank us for our work, and even offered us very generous salaries if we agreed to work with them," Javid says.

That's when the two knew they were fine on their own, that 9-to-5 was never going to be a necessity—or even an option—again, that they didn't *need* it, that creative self-employment was *exactly* where each of them belonged.

When Shining Goes National

Sometimes it feels good to know that your little one-person-that-could business creates for a large client. Denise Dorman felt pretty fabulous when she not only wrote, but also produced, developed and directed a video that aired at The Home Depot locations throughout the United States. "It turned into a major promotion for them, and I won a platinum award," says Dorman.

Jeff Fisher, whom you met in Chapter 8, experienced similar joy when he was approached to write a book. A friend gave him the name and number of an editor, whom he didn't contact until a few months later. When he called, he learned that the editor was no longer with the company. He was then connected to the acquisitions editor. "She immediately said, 'Jeff Fisher, I know who you are. I'd love to work on a book with you,'" says Fisher. "It was a great start to an amazing project."

When he saw his book on the shelves at Powell's City of Books, that was another fond moment. "It's been very gratifying to have several publishers contact me since the release of my first book to write books for them," Fisher says. His next book will be released in 2007.

Christine Miller, an artist and writer from Chapter 9, hit a creative gold when she had her own booth at the National Stationery Show in 2000. "I had my card line for more than four years by that time, so I was somewhat established, but I had never participated in the show with my own booth," Miller says. "I had a fun, beautiful booth surrounded by a lot of other friendly, inspiring artists and the show was a huge success." Her sales were fabulous; she got new license deals and says her presence there really made a statement. "It was, in many ways, the culmination of years of hard work, creating lots of cards, filling hundreds of orders and building a thriving business in a very competitive market."

When It All Just Flows

Billy Bussey, from Chapter 1, doesn't always feel motivated about work, but when a project for one particular client went off without a hitch, he was elated. To this day, he calls on the memory to perk him up when he's not feeling as inspired. He took on a project for the Santa Anita Raceway in California to create a short Flash pre sentation. The purpose of the show was to build excitement for racing. Bussey, who is usually more laidback about his work, took this job seriously. Call it California's good art karma or whatever you want, but his hard work paid off.

"It took us only a week to finish and came out perfect," Bussey says. "The music, which we produced specifically for it, matched perfectly with the flow of the motion graphics, the sound effects and the overall feeling. The 3D animations of horses running and the voiceover script we prepared were not only impressive but entertaining as well. The client loved it. I've never had a project go so smoothly. That was the first time I felt I could handle creative directing efficiently."

All it takes is one taste of success to get your engine revved. And when your enthusiasm or morale settles down—or you face a trial—it's important to remember times of creative success. It reminds us about why we do what we do, because as we've discussed, life as a self-employed creative isn't easy. It's always important to reflect on what we've done and relive our accomplishments. After all, not everyone does what we do.

The Future of Creative Self-Employment

Where do you go now, you may ask? You've seen throughout this book that you're not alone in feeling doubtful, exhilarated, scared and liberated when it comes to creative self-employment. I hope knowing that you are not alone in these feelings brings you motivation to continue on with your creative business, making it—and *you*—stronger than ever.

I hope these stories help you cope when the days are long, short, busy or boring. I hope that the next time you face a difficult time, you'll be able to take a deep breath and think about what you've earned here. I hope you'll remember that it's okay to have a bad day and to doubt yourself from time to time. I hope you can learn ways to get the most out of your job so when hard times come, they won't seem so complicated. I hope you celebrate your successes, and honor the courage you have to do what it is that you do—not everyone can do it!

And I hope you take a step back and look at all you've accomplished—really *see* these successes for the wonderful achievements that they are. Do you remember how you felt before you began living this authentic life, how you hated where you were, how you craved to break free? *You have.* And now you've got some perspective to really enjoy and appreciate what you do.

Because it is, after all, an *extraordinary* life that you lead.

✦

MARKETING- AND BUSINESS-RELATED WEBSITES

www.artofselfpromotion.com
Plenty of tips for promoting yourself for free.

www.creativebusiness.com
Forums, newsletter and a fabulous resource list with organization links.

www.creativity-portal.com
Free articles on a number of issues facing the creatively self-employed.

www.bly.com
Great tips on copywriting and writing that will propel your business further.

www.nolo.com
You don't have to be a legal eagle to get great legal information.

www.marketing.org
Business Marketing Association offers some useful articles on business basics.

www.marketing-mentor.com
Valuable newsletter and free marketing tips.

www.marketingprofs.com
Virtual seminars and useful articles.

www.marketingsherpa.com
Plenty of case studies and logistical how-to's for business success.

www.creativesuccess.com
Articles, useful newsletter and events.

www.creativelatitude.com
Connect with other creatives here and check out useful resources.

www.workingsolo.com
Geared more towards getting your business set up.

www.creativelee.com
Check out the "free stuff" section for tips about organizing and marketing.

www.sba.gov
Small Business Administration's home page, features events and marketing tips.

www.constantcontact.com
E-mail marketing program, features e-mail marketing tips.

www.womma.org
The Word of Mouth Marketing Association site, complete with free tips and event recaps.

www.creativethursday.com
Great podcasts about living the creative life.

Appendix B

✦

Reading List

1. *The 12 Secrets of Highly Creative Women: A Portable Mentor* by Gail McMeekin

2. *Creative Business: Achieving Your Goals Through Creative Thinking and Action* by Chris Genasi and Tim Bills

3. *Creative Colleges: A Guide for Student Actors, Artists, Dancers, Musicians, and Writers* by Elaina Loveland

4. *Freeing the Creative Spirit, Drawing on the Power of Art to Tap the Magic and Wisdom Within* by Adriana Diaz

5. *Go It Alone: The Streetwise Secrets of Self-Employment* by Geoffrey Burch

6. *Guerilla Marketing; Secrets for Making Big Profits from Your Small Business* by Jay Conrad Levinson

7. *Make a Real Living as a Freelance Writer: How to Win Top Writing Assignments* by Jenna Glatzer

8. *Make Your Creative Dreams REAL* by SARK

9. *Refuse to Choose: A Revolutionary Program for Doing Everything You Love* by Barbara Sher

APPENDIX C

✦

CREATIVES' WEBSITES

Zohar Adner:
www.stopstressingout.com

Jackie Alpers:
www.jackiealpers.com

Nancy Ballew:
www.ballewstudio.com

Laurie Barrows:
www.lauriebarrows.com

Holly Becker:
www.decor8.blogspot.com

Ilese Benun:
www.marketing-mentor.com

Tim Benzinger:
www.timbenzinger.com

Denise Biondo:
www.denisebiondo.com

Bob Bly:
www.bly.com

Peter Bowerman:
www.wellfedwriter.com

Sandra Busta:
www.sandrabusta.com

Liz Bywater:
www.bywaterconsultinggroup.com

Billy Bussey:
www.billybussey.com

Ruth Clare:
www.monodesign.com.au

Violette Clark:
www.violette.ca

Stephanie Cockerl:
www.nextsteph.com

Allison Compton:
www.artespy.com

Ben Dattner:
www.dattnerconsulting.com

Joy Deangdeelert:
www.ohjoystudio.com

Alma de la Rosa:
www.thecatspajamasrs.com

Linda Dessau:
www.genuinecoaching.com

Holly DeWolf:
www.sweethappy.ca

ArLyne Diamond:
www.diamondassociates.net

Adriana Diaz:
www.yourcreativelifecoach.com

Kristine DiGrigoli Paige:
www.thesoundandvision.com

Denise Dorman:
www.writebrainmedia.com

Penelope Dullaghan:
www.penelopeillustration.com

Lain Ehmann:
www.knitandpurlgrrl.blogs.com

Beth Erickson:
www.bethannerickson.com

Mike Farley:
www.michaeljmedia.com

Jeff Fisher:
www.jfisherlogomotives.com

Erin Flynn:
www.flynnmedia.com

Ted Forbes:
www.tedforbes.com

Von Glitschka:
www.glitschka.com

Sharon Good:
www.goodlifecoaching.com

Marisa Haedike:
www.creativethursday.com

Celeste Heiter:
www.celesteheiter.com

Claudine Hellmuth:
www.collageartist.com

Andrew Hindes:
www.theinhousewriter.com

Jennifer Hollowell:
www.artistwriter.etsy.com

Kelly James-Enger:
www.becomebodywise.com

Art Javid:
www.graphicwise.com

Liz Kalloch:
www.lizkalloch.com

Michael Katz:
www.bluepenguindevelopment.com

Kristen King:
www.kristenkingfreelancing.com

Cheri Larson:
www.azantejewelry.com

Calvin Lee:
www.mayhemstudios.com

Monica Lee:
www.monicaleestudios.com

Tera Leigh:
www.teraleigh.com

Elaina Loveland:
www.elainaloveland.com

Amy Mantione:
www.elementgraphicdesign.com

Katrina Martin Davenport:
www.kmdavenport.com

Angela Mattson:
www.mattsonbusiness.com

Christine Miller:
www.christinemasonmiller.com

Angela Moore:
www.starfish-pr.com

Catherine Morley:
www.katzidesign.com

Melanie Negrin:
www.merocune.com

Cynthia Potts:
www.cbpotts.net

Craig Poulton:
www.inwebmedia.com

Michael Quinn:
www.powerandgracebook.com

Matt Ramos:
www.mattramosphotography.com

Marianne Roosa:
www.12punt3.nl

M.J. Ryan:
www.mj-ryan.com

Penny Sansevieri:
www.amarketingexpert.com

Patrick Snow:
www.createyourowndestiny.com

Philllis Stacy-Brooks:
www.mainstreetgraphics.com

Mary Stewart-Pellegrini:
www.stewartmanagement.com

Chris Tomlinson:
www.gonink.com

Neil Tortorella:
www.tortorelladesign.com

Kate Voegele:
www.katevoegele.com

Tamar Wallace:
www.tamargraphics.com

Tine Wiggens:
www.tinewiggens.com

Jeff Wilson:
www.jeffwilsonregularguy.com

Evelyn Windley Kaufman:
www.journey2fullness.com

To view a complete list of websites of creatives and experts featured in the book, visit www.creativelyselfemployed.com.

978-0-595-42154-1
0-595-42154-7

Made in the USA